ZERO

THE CASE FOR NUCLEAR WEAPONS ABOLITION

DAVID KRIEGER

A Nuclear Age Peace Foundation Book
1187 Coast Village Road, Suite 1-121
Santa Barbara, California 93108
wagingpeace.org

ISBN: 1478342846
ISBN-13: 9781478342847

Second Edition 2015

David Krieger is a realist. The human race is not sustainable with the clear and present menace of nuclear weapons. Unthinking careerists continue with the pseudorealism of deterrence. But Krieger's wise and urgent book makes an ironclad case for abolition now. In the meantime, we all live with pending vaporization. Any decision to use these genocidal tools cannot and will not be made democratically. The devastation could come from a deranged individual or from a nation-state. In either case, it could still be one person's whim by error, drunkenness, insanity or the "banality of evil." Let us never permit the media to refer to delusional enablers as realists. The call for abolition by David Krieger must be received as a mission by each citizen of this planet. Once accepted, that mission to abolish nuclear weapons will be a prelude to abolishing war.

Blase Bonpane
Co-founder and Director
Office of the Americas

David Krieger has summarized in a heart-rending discourse the reasons why it is imperative for the human race to dismantle its nuclear arsenals. Reason, intellect and sheer emotional imperatives are outlined in this lovely little discourse on the history and the sheer insanity of the nuclear age. Read it and you will be inspired by the imperative to immediately and without delay engage in the most important task that presently faces the human race, indeed all of biological existence—the rapid abolition of all nuclear arsenals led by the powerful and indomitable United States of America.

Helen Caldicott
Australian pediatrician, author
and anti-nuclear activist

My fervent wish is that Barack Obama and Vladimir Putin would read this short book and discover a new meaning to their lives: a mission to use their leadership and power—not later in their lives but now while they are in office, and not with words and "hopes" alone but with new action-policies—to lift the curse of nuclear weapons from the earth. Other readers—leaders, children, parents, voters, activists—whatever else they are doing, will feel that same new added calling as they experience the luminous, quietly passionate prose and poetry of this appeal to humanity.

Daniel Ellsberg
Distinguished Senior Fellow
Nuclear Age Peace Foundation

This excellent book by David Krieger is a must read for those who wish to understand the roots of nuclear weapons and background of their development and proliferation to the nine countries in the "nuclear club." We are reminded of human fallibilities and of the extreme dangers of such omnicidal weapons in our midst. Presidents Obama and Putin would give great hope and leadership to the world if they acted urgently to rid the world of nuclear and other weapons of mass destruction.

Mairead Maguire
Nobel Peace Laureate

With the grace of a poet, logic of a scientist, expertise of a policymaker, skill of a communicator, and passion for life, David Krieger persists with creative tenacity to awaken us all to act urgently to abolish nuclear weapons for human and planetary survival.

Glenn Paige
Chair, Governing Council
Center for Global Nonkilling

Nuclear weapons threaten all of God's creation. Ridding the world of these weapons is our moral responsibility to ourselves, our families, our communities and all life. It is also our responsibility to future generations. We must not wait for another Hiroshima or Nagasaki before we act. This book makes a clear and persuasive case for why we must move urgently and globally to zero nuclear weapons. It should be required reading for all citizens of Earth.

Archbishop Desmond Tutu

Nobel Peace Laureate

"Nuclear weapons are the enemy of humanity."

~ General George Lee Butler

Selected Books by the Author

Speaking of Peace: Quotations to Inspire Action, 2014 (Editor)

The Path to Zero: Dialogues on Nuclear Dangers, 2012 (with Richard Falk)

The Challenge of Abolishing Nuclear Weapons, 2009 (Editor)

At the Nuclear Precipice: Catastrophe or Transformation?, 2008 (Editor, with Richard Falk)

Choose Hope: Your Role in Waging Peace in the Nuclear Age, 2002 (with Daisaku Ikeda)

Nuclear Weapons and the World Court, 1998 (with Ved P. Nanda)

Poetry

Wake Up!, 2015

Summer Grasses: An Anthology of War Poetry, 2014 (Editor)

Never Enough Flowers: The Poetry of Peace II, 2012 (Editor, with Perie Longo)

God's Tears: Reflections on the Atomic Bombs Dropped on Hiroshima and Nagasaki, 2010 (translated to Japanese by Noriko Mizusaki)

The Doves Flew High, 2007

Today Is Not a Good Day for War, 2005

The Poetry of Peace, 2003 (Editor)

Dedicated to all who continue the struggle for a
nuclear weapon-free world, and to the memories
of Albert Camus, Bertrand Russell,
Albert Einstein, Albert Schweitzer,
and Joseph Rotblat

Contents

Acknowledgments

My appreciation to the many colleagues I have worked with over the years who have made the abolition of nuclear weapons their life's work. They are some of the finest and most dedicated people I know. I have learned from them and shared with them the challenges of persevering in speaking truth to power.

My appreciation also to the Board, staff, advisors and members of the Nuclear Age Peace Foundation for believing that we can find a way to end the omnicidal threat that nuclear weapons pose to the human future.

Special thanks to Carol Warner, my assistant, for her good-natured help in preparing the manuscript for publication.

Most of the chapters in this book have appeared in earlier versions as President's Messages on the Nuclear Age Peace Foundation's web site (www.wagingpeace.org), as well as on other sites and in print media.

My appreciation to The Nobel Foundation for permission to include the text of Joseph Rotblat's 1995 Nobel Lecture in this volume.

Some of the poems included in this book have appeared in earlier poetry books I have written, including *God's Tears: Reflections on the Atomic Bombs Dropped on Hiroshima and Nagasaki* (Tokyo: Coal Sack Publishing Company, 2010).

Finally, my appreciation to my wife, Carolee, who has always supported me in the quest to achieve a world without nuclear weapons.

Preface

If we are old enough, we have long memories of the Nuclear Age. In my case, I was born shortly after the US entered into World War II and was three years old when the bombs were dropped on Hiroshima and Nagasaki. I don't specifically remember the bombings, but I do remember the "duck and cover" drills we did in elementary school. The teacher would yell, "Drop," and we were expected to jump quickly under our small desks and curl up with our faces toward the floor. This was the way in which the children of America would be saved from the ravages of an atomic attack. It was a cruel joke. The leaders of the US were prepared to bet the future of civilization and their own children on a nuclear-armed standoff with the Soviet Union in the hope that neither side, by accident or intention, would initiate a nuclear war.

Years later, in the 1990s, a decade or so after I had co-founded the Nuclear Age Peace Foundation, I was invited to speak on a panel on nuclear disarmament that was organized by the Nation Institute. The event was held at my former elementary school, which I hadn't seen since the early 1950s. Before the panel began, I walked to the classroom where I had been a second-grade student. I looked through the small window in the door at the rows of tiny desks and remembered the duck and cover drills we had done. It seemed a very long time ago, and the desks seemed exceedingly small. Children in school no longer do duck and cover drills, but the nuclear dangers that confront us and our children and grandchildren have not gone away.

During the 1950s, bomb shelters were very popular in the United States. There were advertisements for personal bomb shelters that families could install on their properties. Some shelters had thick concrete walls and were buried in the ground. They had ventilation systems that would allow several people to breathe in a small enclosed space. If the shelter were well stocked with food and water, a family could perhaps survive for some weeks or months without emerging into the outdoors.

One evening at dinner when I was about 12 years old, my family discussed bomb shelters. I can remember being surprised by my mother's stance. She said she would never have a bomb shelter. She didn't want to live underground and she didn't like the idea of having to have a gun to keep neighbors from coming into the shelter. She said that she would rather die than live in a bomb shelter. Her attitude, which I hadn't expected, was a powerful lesson in compassion. She was a conscientious objector to the Cold War. She recognized its madness, and was unwilling to buy into saving herself at the expense of humanity. Nine years later, upon my graduation from college, she would offer me a trip to Japan, where I was able to see first-hand what two nuclear weapons had done to the cities of Hiroshima and Nagasaki.

I first visited the cities of Hiroshima and Nagasaki in 1963. Those visits changed my life. The cities were already rebuilt, no longer the flattened expanses of charred debris that they were in the immediate aftermath of the bombings. The vegetation had returned to the cities and there was an air of normalcy. But there were reminders of the bombings throughout the cities and in each city there was a Peace Memorial Museum. At the Peace Memorial Museums, a visitor could not help but be affected by the magnitude of the tragedies, and by what these bombings portended for the human future.

In the United States, the bombings of Hiroshima and Nagasaki were celebrated for bringing an end to World War II, with little concern for the tens of thousands of civilians who lost their lives, some immediately, some over time. The US perspective on the bombings was from above the fray, from the planes carrying the bombs, and from the point of view of the victor. This perspective put us on the path to the development and testing of more atomic weapons and to a mad nuclear arms race. It put all of humanity in danger of annihilation.

One of the best things about traveling is seeing the world from other perspectives. The Peace Memorial Museums in Hiroshima and Nagasaki provided such a perspective, one from beneath the bombs. It was a perspective of the victims, the attacked, those who suffered and died as a result of the bombings.

The survivors of the atomic bombings have a simple message for humanity: "Nuclear weapons and human beings cannot co-exist." We must choose. The survivors, the *hibakusha*, have chosen humanity, and they call upon the people of the world to join them in working to end the nuclear weapons threat to humanity.

Starting with my first visits to Hiroshima and Nagasaki, I became convinced that the survival of humanity is dependent upon the elimination of nuclear weapons. Achieving a nuclear weapon-free world has been my goal throughout my adult life. It was the impetus that moved me to lead in creating the Nuclear Age Peace Foundation in 1982. For over three decades, I have worked with some of the most dedicated and amazing people on the planet—people who are committed to assuring that humanity has a future free of the threat of nuclear annihilation. The Nuclear Age Peace Foundation has grown from its five founders to over 70,000 members today.

The mission of the Foundation is to educate and advocate for peace and a world free of nuclear weapons, and to empower peace leaders. To achieve a world free of nuclear weapons is the greatest challenge of our time. It is our obligation today, as it was for previous generations, to pass the world on intact to new generations. Never before in human history have the stakes been higher or the challenge greater.

ZERO

THE CASE FOR NUCLEAR WEAPONS ABOLITION

The Final Period?

Scientists have given us a creation story. They tell us that the universe was created with a "Big Bang" some 13.7 billion years ago. To comprehend this enormous stretch of time, we can round off to 15 billion years and imagine a 15,000-page book. It would be a very large and heavy book, some 50 times larger than an average 300-page book. In this book, each page would represent one million years in the history of the universe. If there were 1,000 words on each page, each word would represent 1,000 years.

Most of the book would be about the expansion of the universe after the Big Bang. Our solar system would not occur in this history of the universe until page 10,500. It would take another 700 pages until the first primitive forms of life would appear on Earth some 3.8 billion years ago, and the slow evolution of life would fill the book to its end. Not until page 14,997 would our earliest human ancestors appear on the planet. Homo sapiens would not appear until 200 words before the book's end, and would not begin to spread beyond Africa until 70 words before the book's end. Agricultural societies would show up just 12 words before the end of the volume, and large-scale human civilizations would make their appearances just five or six words from the end of page 15,000.

The Nuclear Age, which began in 1945, would be represented by the final punctuation mark on the last page of the 15,000-page book. It might be a period, a question mark or an exclamation point. This small mark at the end of the volume indicates where we are today: inheritors of a 13.7-billion-year history, with the capacity to destroy ourselves and most other forms of life with our technological "achievements." It is up to us—those of us alive on the planet now—to assure that the page is turned, and that we move safely into the future, free from the threat that nuclear weapons pose to humanity and other forms of life.

Hiroshima and Nagasaki

By August 1945, most Japanese cities had been leveled by US bombing raids with conventional bombs. The Japanese had virtually no air defenses left to protect their cities. However, Hiroshima and Nagasaki and two other Japanese cities had been kept largely off-limits to the US Army Air Corps by US war planners. These cities were being saved for atomic weapons. The US didn't want to use its atomic weapons to bomb cities that had already been reduced to rubble. It wanted the weapons to make a powerful impression on Japanese leaders.

In April 1945, President Franklin Delano Roosevelt died, and Vice President Harry Truman assumed the presidency. Truman did not know about the US atomic bomb program until shortly after becoming president when he was briefed by Secretary of War Henry Stimson. Truman did not directly make a decision to use the atomic bombs; rather, he didn't stop the plans to use them from moving forward.[1]

The US government had broken the Japanese diplomatic code and knew that Japan was trying to surrender. A number of Truman's advisors with knowledge of Japan told him that the Japanese would surrender if he would alter the US position of "unconditional surrender" to allow the Japanese to keep their emperor. In fact, when Truman sailed for a summit of the Allied leaders at Potsdam in July 1945, a draft statement he carried aboard the *USS Augusta* contained a clause in Article 12 allowing the Japanese emperor to remain following Japan's surrender.[2]

Truman traveled to Europe with Secretary of State Jimmy Byrnes, who had strong feelings about both unconditional surrender and the use of the bomb. Byrnes believed that if the American people learned that the US had poured financial and scientific resources into creating the bomb and then didn't use it to end the war as soon as possible, the Democrats would be punished in the next election. When Truman arrived in Europe, the clause about allowing the emperor to remain was no longer in his draft statement.[3]

While in Potsdam, Truman learned of the successful US test of a nuclear device at Alamogordo, New Mexico. It seemed to have changed Truman's outlook and to have given him more confidence, particularly in his relations with Soviet leader Joseph Stalin. He bragged to Stalin about having a new, powerful weapon. Stalin, through reports of spies, already knew about the weapon and had begun a Soviet project to create its own atomic weapons.[4]

After the war in Europe ended on May 8, 1945, the US was eager for the Soviets to join them in finishing the war in the Pacific. Stalin had agreed to enter the war in the Pacific three months after the end of the war in Europe, putting the date at around August 8, 1945. By mid-July, however, the US was no longer so interested in sharing the spoils of victory in the Pacific war. Plans were made to use the two nuclear weapons in the US arsenal before the Soviets entered the Pacific war, or at least before they could move their troops very far into the Pacific theater.

In the early morning hours of August 6, 1945, a US B-29 bomber left Tinian Island in the Pacific and flew toward Japan. Its target was the city of Hiroshima. The plane, named *Enola Gay*, arrived over its target at around 8:15 a.m. and released its single atomic bomb. The bomb fell from the plane for 43 seconds before exploding some 580 meters above the city. The temperature at the hypocenter exceeded a million degrees centigrade. The heat and blast destroyed virtually everything within a radius of approximately a mile from the epicenter. The bomb also started fires and the wooden houses were tinder for fueling the fires. Shadows were left on walls where humans were incinerated by the heat of the explosion. The city was leveled, with only a small number of its buildings left standing.

Some 90,000 people perished that day in Hiroshima. More would die in the subsequent months due to the injuries they suffered and the radiation poisoning from the atomic explosion. By the end of 1945, some 145,000 people had died from the bombing of Hiroshima. Although Truman said that the US had bombed a military target, in fact the US had bombed the center of the city. Those who died in Hiroshima were overwhelmingly civilians—children, women and the elderly.

Truman was sailing home from the Potsdam conference on the *USS Augusta* when he was given the news of the bombing of Hiroshima. He made the unfortunate remark, "This is the greatest thing in history."[5]

Three days after the destruction of Hiroshima, a second US atomic bombing mission set out from Tinian Island. This time the target was the city of Kokura on the Japanese island of Kyushu. When the plane, a B-29 named *Bockscar*, arrived at Kokura, the city was clouded over and the crew was unable to find its target for the bomb. Consequently, the bomber flew on to its secondary target, the city of Nagasaki. This city was also clouded over, but a break in the clouds allowed the crew to release its plutonium powered bomb over the city. This bomb claimed some 40,000 lives immediately and a total of some 75,000 lives by the end of 1945.

GOD RESPONDED WITH TEARS

The plane flew over Hiroshima and dropped the bomb
after the all clear warning had sounded.

The bomb dropped far slower than the speed of light.
It dropped at the speed of bombs.

From the ground it was a tiny silver speck
that separated from the silver plane.

After 43 seconds, the slow falling bomb exploded
into mass at the speed of light squared.

Einstein called it energy. Everything lit up.
For a split-second people could see their own bones.

The pilot always believed he had done the right thing.
The President, too, never wavered from his belief.

He thanked God for the bomb. Others did, too.
God responded with tears that fell far slower

than the speed of bombs.
They still have not reached Earth.

Were the Atomic
Bombings Necessary?

On August 14, 1945, Japan surrendered and World War II was over. American policy makers have argued that the atomic bombs were the precipitating cause of the surrender. Historical studies of the Japanese decision, however, reveal that what the Japanese were most concerned with was the Soviet Union's entry into the war. Japan surrendered with the understanding that the emperor system would be retained. The US agreed to do what Truman had been advised to do before the bombings, signaling to the Japanese that they would be allowed to retain the emperor.[6] This has left historians to speculate that the war could have ended without either the use of the two atomic weapons on Japanese cities or an Allied invasion of Japan.

The US Strategic Bombing Survey concluded that, even without the use of the atomic bombs, without the Soviet Union entering the war and without an Allied invasion of Japan, the war would have ended before December 31, 1945 and, in all likelihood, before November 1, 1945.[7] Prior to the use of the atomic bombs on Hiroshima and Nagasaki, the US was destroying Japanese cities at will with conventional bombs. The Japanese were offering virtually no resistance. The US dropped atomic bombs on a nation that had been largely defeated and some of whose leaders were seeking terms of surrender.

Despite strong evidence that the atomic bombings were not responsible for ending the war with Japan, most Americans, particularly those who lived through World War II, believe that they were. Many World War II era servicemen who were in the Pacific or anticipated being shipped there believed that the bombs saved them from fighting hard battles on the shores of Japan, as had been fought on the islands of Iwo Jima and Okinawa. What they did not take into account was that the Japanese were trying to surrender, that the US had broken the Japanese codes and knew they were trying to surrender, and that, had the US accepted their offer, the war could have ended without the use of the atomic bombs.

Most high ranking Allied military leaders were appalled by the use of the atomic bombs. General Eisenhower, the Supreme Commander of Allied Forces Europe, recognized that Japan was ready to surrender and said, "It wasn't necessary to hit them with that awful thing."[8] General Hap Arnold, commander of the US Army Air Corps, pointed out, "Atomic bomb or no atomic bomb, the Japanese were already on the verge of collapse."[9]

Admiral William Leahy, Truman's chief of staff, put it this way: "The use of this barbarous weapon at Hiroshima and Nagasaki was of no material assistance in our war against Japan. The Japanese were already defeated and ready to surrender. In being the first to use it, we adopted an ethical standard common to barbarians of the Dark Ages. Wars cannot be won by destroying women and children."[10]

What Truman had described as "the greatest thing in history" was actually, according to his own military leaders, an act of unparalleled cowardice, the mass annihilation of men, women and children. The use of the atomic bombs was the culmination of an air war fought against civilians in Germany and Japan, an air war that showed increasing contempt for the lives of civilians and for the laws of war.

The end of the war was a great relief to those who had fought for so long. There were nuclear scientists, though, who now regretted what they had created and how their creations had been used. One of these was Leo Szilard, the Hungarian émigré physicist who had warned Einstein of the possibility of the Germans creating an atomic weapon first and of the need for the US to begin a bomb project. Szilard had convinced Einstein to send a letter of warning to Roosevelt, which led at first to a small project to explore the potential of uranium to sustain a chain reaction and then to the Manhattan Project that resulted in the creation of the first atomic weapons.[11]

Szilard did his utmost to prevent the bomb from being used against Japanese civilians. He wanted to meet with Roosevelt, but before he could, on April 12, 1945, the president died. Szilard next tried to meet with the new president, Harry Truman, but Truman sent him to Spartanburg, South Carolina to talk with Truman's mentor in the Senate, Jimmy Byrnes, who was dismissive of Szilard. Szilard then tried to organize the scientists in the Manhattan Project to appeal for a demonstration of the bomb rather than immediately using it on a Japanese city. The appeal was stalled by General Leslie Groves, the head of the Manhattan Project, and did not reach President Truman until after the atomic bombs were used.[12]

The use of the bomb caused many other scientists to despair as well. Albert Einstein deeply regretted that he had written to President Roosevelt. Einstein did not work on the Manhattan Project, but he had used his influence to encourage the start of the American bomb project. Einstein, like

Szilard, believed that the purpose of the US bomb project was to deter the use of a German bomb. He was shocked that, once created, the bomb was used offensively against the Japanese. Einstein would spend the remaining ten years of his life speaking out against the bomb and seeking its elimination. He famously said, "The unleashed power of the atom has changed everything except our modes of thinking, and thus we drift toward unparalleled catastrophe."[13]

EISENHOWER'S VIEW

*"It wasn't necessary to hit them
with that awful thing."*
~ General Dwight D. Eisenhower

We hit them with it, first
at Hiroshima and then at Nagasaki –
the old one-two punch.

The bombings were tests really, to see
what those "awful things" would do.

First, of a gun-type uranium bomb, and then
of a plutonium implosion bomb.

Both proved highly effective
in the art of obliterating cities.

It wasn't necessary.

One *Hibakusha*

Hibakusha is the Japanese word for those who survived the atomic bombings of Hiroshima and Nagasaki. Miyoko Matsubara was 13 years old when the first US atomic bomb used in warfare was dropped on the city of Hiroshima. She worked that morning clearing debris with other students in her middle school class. She looked at the sky and saw an airplane flying overhead from which emerged a small silver speck. It was the bomb the Americans called "Little Boy," a uranium gun-type atomic weapon. It descended for 43 seconds and then exploded 580 meters above the city. Miyoko was thrown to the ground and rendered unconscious. This is what she remembered of that day:

> *I had no idea how long I had lain unconscious, but when I regained consciousness the bright sunny morning had turned into night. Takiko, who had stood next to me, had simply disappeared from my sight. I could see none of my friends nor any other students. Perhaps they had been blown away by the blast.*

I rose to my feet surprised. All that was left of my jacket was the upper part around my chest. And my baggy working trousers were gone, leaving only the waistband and a few patches of cloth. The only clothes left on me were dirty white underwear.

Then I realized that my face, hands, and legs had been burned, and were swollen with the skin peeled off and hanging down in shreds. I was bleeding and some areas had turned yellow. Terror struck me, and I felt that I had to go home. And the next moment, I frantically started running away from the scene forgetting all about the heat and pain.

On my way home, I saw a lot of people. All of them were almost naked and looked like characters out of horror movies with their skin and flesh horribly burned and blistered. The place around the Tsurumi bridge was crowded with many injured people. They held their arms aloft in front of them. Their hair stood on end. They were groaning and cursing. With pain in their eyes and furious looks on their faces, they were crying out for their mothers to help them.

I was feeling unbearably hot, so I went down to the river. There were a lot of people in the water crying and shouting for help. Countless dead bodies were being carried away by the water—some floating, some sinking. Some bodies had been badly hurt, and their intestines were exposed. It was a horrible sight, yet I had to jump in the water to save myself from heat I felt all over.[14]

Some 50 years later, Miyoko would come to Santa Barbara to visit the Nuclear Age Peace Foundation. She was a humble woman who bowed deeply. She worked hard to learn English so that she could tell her story and awaken young people to the threat of nuclear weapons. She wanted to assure that her past would not become their future. Her story is the story of many *hibakusha*. If people everywhere could hear Miyoko's story, nuclear weapons would be known for what they are: indiscriminate devices of mass annihilation.

THE DEEP BOW OF A *HIBAKUSHA*

for Miyoko Matsubara

She bowed deeply. She bowed deeper than the oceans. She bowed from the top of Mt. Fuji to the bottom of the ocean. She bowed so deeply and so often that the winds blew hard.

The winds blew her whispered apologies and prayers across all the continents. But the winds whistled too loudly, and made it impossible to hear her apologies and prayers. The winds made the oceans crazy. The water in the oceans rose up in a wild molecular dance. The oceans threw themselves against the continents. The people were frightened. They ran screaming from the shores. They feared the white water and the whistling wind. They huddled together in dark places. They strained to hear the words in the wind.

In some places there were some people who thought they heard an apology. In other places there were people who thought they heard a prayer.

She bowed deeply. She bowed more deeply than anyone should bow.

An Unprecedented Challenge

Nuclear weapons are capable of destroying the human species along with most other forms of life on the planet. That is what separates the Nuclear Age from the long stretch of history that precedes it. Humans have always been capable of committing, and have committed, homicide and genocide. But in the Nuclear Age we have become capable of *omnicide*, the death of all. Since the risks of human annihilation are greater than ever before in human history, the responsibility to prevent this from occurring is commensurately greater.

In a world with enough nuclear weapons to destroy complex life on the planet many times over, how are we to fulfill our responsibility to pass on the planet intact to new generations? Often when speaking out for a world free of nuclear weapons, we are met with massive indifference and complacency. Many people on the planet would prefer not to have the means of nuclear annihilation, but many others believe they are safer with these weapons than without them. The basis for this belief is the myth that nuclear weapons provide security by means of nuclear deterrence. That is, they believe that nuclear weapons provide protection to those who possess them by the threat of nuclear retaliation if attacked. Their understanding is that nuclear deterrence is a shield that will protect them from harm. Of course, in reality these weapons are not a shield.

Nuclear deterrence derives from psychological and communications hypotheses about human behavior. To work as posited, nuclear deterrence requires that the threat of retaliation be communicated to a potential attacker, that it be believed by the potential attacker, and that the potential attacker exhibit rational behavior in refraining from attack due to fear of retaliation. None of this is guaranteed to work. People think differently. Leaders are not always rational. There are circumstances, particularly under conditions of stress, when any leader is subject to behaving irrationally.

The first atomic weapons were used in August 1945 to destroy the Japanese cities of Hiroshima and Nagasaki. Since then, nuclear weapons have not been used in warfare, although there have been many occasions in which they might have been used. The United States did not use nuclear weapons to prevent a stalemate in Korea or to escape defeat in Vietnam. The former Soviet Union did not use nuclear weapons to prevent defeat in Afghanistan. Other nuclear-armed nations have also used nuclear restraint in other wars. But does this mean that these weapons will never be used again? There are no guarantees.

Martin E. Hellman, Professor Emeritus of Electrical Engineering at Stanford University and an expert in risk analysis, estimates that there is greater than a ten percent chance of a child born today not living out his natural lifetime due to nuclear war, and he believes it is possible that the risk could be as great as 50 percent.[15] These are not comforting odds. Nuclear weapons are a real and present danger; unfortunately, they are not being treated as such.

Too many people are complacent, viewing nuclear arms as a low-priority issue or one that went away with the end of the Cold War. But there are still approximately 16,000 nuclear weapons in the world, and just under 2,000 of these in the arsenals of the US and Russia remain on high-alert status, ready to be fired within moments of an order to do so.[16] The use of these weapons, by accident or design, could destroy the progress of civilization over the past 10,000 years and send the world spinning into another Dark Age.

Humankind, by its scientific genius, has created tools capable of causing its demise. Our challenge is to react to this situation with the mature intelligence needed for dealing with the problem. If we go on with business as usual, we leave our survival to chance. Many people think about nuclear weapons in this way: "The genie is out of the bottle and can't be put back inside." This is defeatist thinking. It suggests that there is little that can be done but to await our fate. Instead, this is a time to work together with other countries to do exactly what the pessimists say cannot be done. We must put the genie back in the bottle. This will require leadership.

The country that should lead the effort to achieve a nuclear weapon-free world is the United States. It is the world's most militarily powerful country, and without its leadership other key countries won't join the effort. This does not mean that the US should disarm its nuclear arsenal unilaterally. Rather, it should work with other countries to diminish the role of nuclear weapons in their military strategies while negotiating the phased, verifiable, irreversible and transparent elimination of nuclear weapons everywhere.

There is another reason why it is appropriate for the US to lead the global effort to eliminate nuclear weapons. As the country that initiated the Nuclear Age and as the only country that has ever used nuclear weapons in war, the US should seize the opportunity to lead the way out. President Obama took note of this responsibility in his April 2009 speech in Prague (see Appendix A). He said, "...as the only nuclear power to have used a nuclear weapon, the United States has a moral responsibility to act. We cannot succeed in this endeavor alone, but we can lead it, we can start it."[17]

The US has the capacity to lead the way to a world without nuclear weapons. The US itself would be far safer in such a world. Right now the only weapons that threaten US cities and even the existence of the US as a political entity are nuclear weapons. US politicians and military leaders should be working day and night on developing a path to zero nuclear weapons. Unfortunately, they are not doing so.

In his Prague speech, President Obama also said, "I state clearly and with conviction America's commitment to seek the peace and security of a world without nuclear weapons."[18] It was a powerful statement for which he received strong applause and later a Nobel Peace Prize. Unfortunately, he followed this statement by one with a dampening effect. "I'm not naïve," he said. "This goal will not be reached quickly—perhaps not in my lifetime."[19] As President Obama is a relatively young man, that would put the goal somewhere in the far future and suggests that it is one that lacks urgency. "It will take patience and persistence,"[20] the President insisted. It will, but it also will require a sense of urgency if it is to be achieved.

Nuclear Weapon States

Nine countries possess nuclear weapons: the United States, Russia, United Kingdom, France, China, Israel, India, Pakistan and North Korea. Over ninety percent of the world's nuclear weapons are in the arsenals of the US and Russia. These two countries must help lead the way toward a world without nuclear weapons. But the US must take the first step, for if it does not then Russia will not reduce its nuclear arsenal and if Russia does not then China will not, and so on with all countries possessing nuclear weapons.

All nuclear weapon states have reasons to justify their nuclear arsenals. They argue that nuclear weapons and the threat to use these weapons in retaliation make them more secure. It may be, though, that nuclear deterrence, which has been so heavily relied upon by the nuclear weapon states, will not work under certain circumstances. The belief in nuclear deterrence is a belief in a false idol.

As stated earlier, nuclear deterrence cannot provide physical protection to a nuclear-armed country. It provides only a psychological barrier. It requires that a potential attacker believe that the targeted country has the capability and the intention to retaliate. A leader may believe that such intent must be regularly demonstrated through nuclear weapon and missile tests. The intent to retaliate must also be believed by a potential attacker. Nuclear deterrence could fail if an attacker believed that the intent to retaliate was absent. Of course, it would be a very risky gamble, like playing Russian roulette.

Nuclear deterrence also requires rationality. For the theory of deterrence to work, a potential nuclear attacker must think and act rationally. Knowing that there will be retaliation for a nuclear attack, the potential attacker is likely to refrain from attacking. But if the potential attacker is not rational, he may attack anyway. He may be paranoid or suicidal. He may not care about inciting a retaliatory attack. If so, nuclear deterrence will fail.

Nuclear deterrence will fail against a terrorist organization that cannot be located. If a terrorist organization obtains a nuclear weapon, the threat of retaliation will be useless. There will be nowhere to retaliate. Terrorists may also be suicidal, which is yet another reason why there must be zero tolerance for terrorists obtaining nuclear weapons. Achieving the goal of zero tolerance will require achieving the goal of zero nuclear weapons.

Concerns about the effectiveness of nuclear deterrence led to an arms race between the US and Russia that at its height in 1986 resulted in a combined total of some 70,000 nuclear weapons. Thankfully, this number has come down, but at approximately 16,000 it is still far too high.

When nuclear weapon states rely upon nuclear weapons for deterrence they are setting the worst possible example for the other states in the world. They are saying, in effect, that nuclear weapons make them more secure. When the militarily strongest states in the world are perceived to rely upon nuclear weapons for their security, they create incentive for other states to develop their own nuclear arsenals. In other words, nuclear weapons possession promotes nuclear weapons proliferation.

Controlling the Bomb

The US emerged from World War II as the sole possessor of the atomic bomb. It had demonstrated that it was willing to use these weapons to serve its own interests. President Truman believed that it would take decades for another country to develop atomic weapons, but the scientists knew better. They predicted that it would be only a few years before the Soviet Union would have its own bomb. The scientists were correct. It took just four years. The US monopoly on nuclear weapons was ended with the first Soviet nuclear weapon test on August 29, 1949.

The United Nations Charter was signed on June 23, 1945. It contained no reference to atomic weapons, as the use of the weapons had not yet taken place. When the United Nations General Assembly met for the first time in early 1946, however, its members were well aware of the destructive power of nuclear weapons. The very first resolution of the UN General Assembly in January 1946 established a commission to deal with the problems raised by atomic energy. In the terms of reference for the Commission, it was asked to make specific proposals:

(a) for extending between all nations the exchange of basic scientific information for peaceful ends;

(b) for control of atomic energy to the extent necessary to ensure its use only for peaceful purposes;

(c) *for the elimination from national armaments of atomic weapons and of all other major weapons adaptable to mass destruction;*

(d) for effective safeguards by way of inspection and other means to protect complying States against the hazards of violation and evasions. The work of the Commission should proceed by separate stages, the successful completion of each of which will develop the necessary confidence of the world before the next stage is undertaken.[21] (Emphasis added.)

Some early attempts were made to bring the bomb under international control. The Acheson-Lilienthal Plan was presented to the United Nations by US financier Bernard Baruch. The Plan called for international control of atomic energy. As presented by Baruch, the plan would have required inspections of the Soviet Union before the US weapons were placed under international control.[22] The Soviet Union presented an alternative plan that sought US nuclear disarmament before national inspections. Agreement could not be reached, and the stage was set for the nuclear arms race that followed. By 1952 the US had succeeded in developing thermonuclear weapons, far more powerful than the weapons that destroyed Hiroshima and Nagasaki. A year later, in 1953, the Soviets also tested a thermonuclear weapon. Both sides had taken a quantum leap in their capacity for annihilation.

A Short History Lesson
and a Hypothetical Scenario

H iroshima was destroyed by a US atomic bomb on August 6, 1945. Three days later, on August 9, 1945, Nagasaki was destroyed by another US atomic bomb. In between these bombings, on August 8, 1945, the US signed the *Charter of the Nuremberg Tribunal*, in which the Allied powers agreed to hold the leaders of the Axis powers to account for crimes against peace, war crimes and crimes against humanity.[23] The irony and hypocrisy of this should not be lost on history. It was a crime under international humanitarian law then, as it is now, to attack and slaughter a civilian population. That is what the US did at Hiroshima and again at Nagasaki, while preparing to hold others accountable for crimes under international law. It is perhaps the reason why President Truman declared to the world that the US had attacked "a military base," rather than a city of mostly civilians, at Hiroshima.

To place the crimes of the nuclear attacks on Hiroshima and Nagasaki in context, it is useful to imagine a hypothetical scenario in which the Nazis had succeeded in developing three atomic weapons before the US did. Let us further imagine that the Nazis had tested one of the weapons, as the US did, and then used the other two weapons to attack two cities in the UK, say London and Coventry. Now, imagine that the Germans had somehow still gone on to lose the war against the Allied powers, and its leaders were brought before the Nuremberg Tribunal to be held to account for crimes committed under international law. It is impossible to imagine in this scenario that the Nazi leaders would not have been tried, convicted and severely punished for using the atomic weapons on two undefended cities.

In this hypothetical scenario, the world would have viewed the use of nuclear weapons very differently. The use of these weapons would have been understood to be criminal acts by deranged leaders as opposed to being perceived as having saved lives and ending a long and terrible war. The lesson from this hypothetical seems to be that, if you are going to commit heinous crimes under international law during a war, you must be sure to win the war so you can avoid judgment. The US leaders during World War II did this, but they cannot escape the judgment of history.

A SHORT HISTORY LESSON: 1945

August 6th:
Dropped atomic bomb
On civilians
At Hiroshima.

August 8th:
Agreed to hold
War crimes trials
For Nazis.

August 9th:
Dropped atomic bomb
On civilians
At Nagasaki.

The Responsibility of Scientists

Nuclear weapons were first created by scientists and engineers working in the US nuclear weapons program, the Manhattan Project, during World War II. Nuclear weapons are unique among weapons systems—they are capable of destroying civilization and possibly the human species. Nuclear weapons kill massively and indiscriminately. They are insanely powerful. They are also illegal, immoral and cowardly. They are long-distance killing machines, instruments of annihilation. They place the human future in jeopardy. In spite of all of this, or perhaps perversely because of it, these weapons seem to bestow prestige upon their creators and possessors.

By examining the reflections of three leading scientists whose early work involved them in significant ways with the creation of nuclear weapons, I will show how they set an example for scientists today. I will seek to answer these questions: Do the scientists who created nuclear weapons have special responsibility for these weapons? Do scientists today continue to have responsibility for nuclear weapons?

Albert Einstein

Albert Einstein was one of the greatest men of the 20th century, and one of the people I most admire. His penetrating intellect changed our view of the universe. His understanding of the relationship between mass and energy, as contained in his famous equation $E=mc^2$, was the original theoretical insight into the power of mass converted to energy. Einstein, however, for all his theoretical brilliance, did not initially foresee the potential power that would be released by the atom and give rise to nuclear weapons.

By 1939 Einstein was living in the United States as a refugee from Hitler's Germany, and he had a position at Princeton's Institute for Advanced Study. A fellow physicist and friend, Leo Szilard, a Hungarian refugee from Nazi Germany, became concerned that the Germans would develop an atomic weapon and use it to threaten or defeat the other countries standing in Hitler's way. Szilard, with fellow scientist Eugene Wigner, went to Einstein and expressed his fear. He asked Einstein to sign a letter explaining the danger to President Franklin Roosevelt. The letter that Einstein sent said that "uranium may turn into a new and important source of energy in the immediate future," and that, while not certain, "extremely powerful bombs of a new type may be constructed." The letter called upon President Roosevelt to have his administration maintain contact with "a group of physicists working on chain reactions in America."[24] The letter led Roosevelt to take the first steps toward what would become the Manhattan Project, a very large, secret US government program to create atomic weapons. President Roosevelt set up an Advisory Committee on Uranium, headed by Lyman J. Briggs, to evaluate where the US stood with regard to uranium research and to recommend what role the US government should play.[25]

Einstein never worked on the Manhattan Project to make the atomic bomb, and he was deeply disturbed and saddened when the bombs were used on Japan. He was reported to have said later, "If only I had known, I should have become a watchmaker."[26]

During the final ten years of his life after the bombs were used, Einstein would join and lend his name to many organizations working to control and eliminate nuclear weapons. In 1946, Einstein joined the Emergency Committee of Atomic Scientists. At the end of a conference held in Princeton in November 1946, Einstein and his fellow trustees of the Emergency Committee released a statement that included the following "facts...accepted by all scientists":

Atomic bombs can now be made cheaply and in large number. They will become more destructive.

There is no military defense against the atomic bomb and none is to be expected.

Other nations can rediscover our secret processes by themselves.

Preparedness against atomic war is futile, and if attempted will ruin the structure of our social order.

If war breaks out, atomic bombs will be used and they will surely destroy our civilization.

There is no solution to this problem except international control of atomic energy and, ultimately, the elimination of war.[27]

These six points remain as valid today as they were in 1946. The last public statement that Einstein signed, just days before his death, was the Russell-Einstein Manifesto (see Appendix B). He sent a letter to Bertrand Russell indicating his support of the Manifesto and his agreement with Russell's choice of other prospective signers. The Russell-Einstein Manifesto is one of the most powerful anti-nuclear and anti-war statements ever written. The document begins, "In the tragic situation that confronts humanity, we feel that scientists should assemble in conference to appraise the perils that have arisen as a result of the development of weapons of mass destruction, and to discuss a resolution in the spirit of the appended draft."[28]

The Manifesto expresses the fear of massive destruction made possible by nuclear weapons that could bring an end to the human species. It states: "Here, then, is the problem which we present to you, stark and dreadful and inescapable: Shall we put an end to the human race; or shall mankind renounce war?"[29] Einstein and Russell were joined by nine other prominent scientists in calling upon people everywhere, and particularly scientists, to take a simple but critical step: "Remember your humanity, and forget the rest."[30]

Leo Szilard

Leo Szilard was another remarkable scientist of the 20th century. He first conceived of the possibility of an atomic chain reaction that could result in atomic bombs while standing at a stoplight in London in 1933.[31] One of the people Szilard credits with influencing his discovery was British novelist H.G. Wells, who wrote about atomic bombs in his 1913 science fiction book, *The Last War, A World Set Free.*[32]

Six years after conceiving of the scientific possibility of an atomic bomb, it would be Szilard who would encourage

Einstein to warn President Roosevelt about the possibility of a German atomic bomb. After the Manhattan Project was underway, Szilard would work with Enrico Fermi at the University of Chicago on creating a controlled chain reaction. The two men succeeded in conducting the first controlled and sustained chain reaction in their laboratory under the bleachers at the University of Chicago on December 2, 1942. In doing so, they left no doubt that creation of an atomic weapon would be possible.[33]

By early 1945, it seemed clear to Szilard that Germany would not succeed in creating an atomic bomb, but that America would. Szilard became concerned that the US would choose to use its new weapon as an instrument of war rather than as a means of deterring the German use of an atomic weapon. Szilard made frantic attempts to stop the US from using the bomb that he had been so instrumental in creating. He went back to Einstein in an attempt to arrange a meeting with President Roosevelt. Einstein wrote another letter to Roosevelt on Szilard's behalf. The President's wife, Eleanor Roosevelt, wrote back agreeing to meet with Szilard in her Manhattan apartment. Szilard received the letter with great excitement, but his excitement was dashed when later in the day it was announced that President Roosevelt was dead.[34]

Next, Szilard tried to arrange a meeting with the new president, Harry Truman. Truman arranged for Szilard to meet with Jimmy Byrnes, a Senate mentor of Truman who would soon be named his Secretary of State. Szilard, along with scientists Walter Bartky and Harold Urey, traveled to Spartanburg, South Carolina to meet with Byrnes. Szilard made an unfavorable impression on Byrnes, and the meeting went badly. Szilard expressed concern about a nuclear arms race with the Soviet Union, but Byrnes seemed to be more concerned with the possibility of using the new weapon as a demonstration of military might to make the Soviets more manageable. Szilard later wrote, "I was rarely as depressed as when we left Byrnes's house and walked to the station."[35]

Szilard next worked energetically on the Committee on Political and Social Problems composed of scientists working on the bomb at the University of Chicago. The Committee was headed by Nobel Laureate physicist James Franck. The Committee Report concluded that the bomb should be demonstrated to Japan before being used against Japanese civilians.[36] The Scientific Committee of the Manhattan Project's Interim Committee—composed of Arthur Holly Compton, Enrico Fermi, Ernest O. Lawrence and Robert Oppenheimer—rejected the Report, recommending against a demonstration and for military use of the bomb.[37]

Finally, Szilard drafted a petition to the President of the United States. The petition, dated July 17, 1945, began, "Discoveries of which the people of the United States are not aware may affect the welfare of this nation in the near future...."[38] The petition argued against attacking Japanese civilians on moral and practical grounds. It argued that "a nation which sets a precedent of using these newly liberated forces of nature for purposes of destruction may have to bear the responsibility of opening the door to an era of devastation on an unimaginable scale."[39] The petition was held by General Leslie Groves, the head of the Manhattan Project, and did not reach Secretary of Defense Stimson or President Truman until after Hiroshima had been destroyed by the first attack with a nuclear weapon.

After the war, Szilard was a leader among atomic scientists working to alert the public to nuclear dangers. He was a founder of the Council for a Livable World. He remained active in opposing nuclear weapons until his death in 1964.

The Responsibility of Scientists

Joseph Rotblat

The third important scientist of the 20th century to take a leadership role for abolishing nuclear weapons was Joseph Rotblat, a Polish émigré who went to London in 1939 to work with Nobel Laureate physicist James Chadwick. Rotblat became concerned about a German atomic weapon, which led him to work on the British atomic bomb project and later on the US Manhattan Project. Like Szilard, he believed that an Allied atomic bomb was necessary to deter Germany from using its possible atomic bomb. By late 1944, however, Rotblat had concluded that the Germans would not succeed in creating an atomic weapon. He was shocked to hear from General Groves one evening that the purpose of the US bomb project had always been for leverage against the Soviet Union, a country that was then a US ally in the war. As an act of conscience, Rotblat left the Manhattan Project in December 1944 and returned to London.[40] The following August his worst fears were realized when the US used its newly created weapons at Hiroshima and Nagasaki.

Rotblat would dedicate the rest of his life to working for a nuclear weapon-free world. He collaborated in the creation of the 1955 Russell-Einstein Manifesto, and was its youngest signer. Two years later, he helped organize the first meeting of the Pugwash Conferences on Science and World Affairs, bringing together scientists from East and West. He would serve as a leader of the Pugwash movement for the rest of his long life, always as a voice of conscience and reason and a strong and uncompromising advocate of nuclear weapons abolition. He was the living embodiment of the Russell-Einstein Manifesto, calling for nuclear weapons abolition and the abolition of war.

In 1995, Joseph Rotblat received the Nobel Peace Prize. As part of his Nobel Lecture (see Appendix C), he appealed to his fellow scientists. In doing so, he referred approvingly to the statement made earlier that year by former Manhattan Project scientist Hans Bethe on the 50th anniversary of the Hiroshima bombing, and he quoted Bethe's statement in full:

As the Director of the Theoretical Division at Los Alamos, I participated at the most senior level in the World War II Manhattan Project that produced the first atomic weapons.

Now, at age 88, I am one of the few remaining such senior persons alive. Looking back at the half century since that time, I feel the most intense relief that these weapons have not been used since World War II, mixed with the horror that tens of thousands of such weapons have been built since that time—one hundred times more than any of us at Los Alamos could ever have imagined.

Today we are rightly in an era of disarmament and dis-mantlement of nuclear weapons. But in some countries nuclear weapons development still continues. Whether and when the various Nations of the World can agree to stop this is uncertain. But individual scientists can still influ-ence this process by withholding their skills.

Accordingly, I call on all scientists in all countries to cease and desist from work creating, developing, improving and manufacturing further nuclear weapons—and, for that matter, other weapons of potential mass destruction such as chemical and biological weapons.[41]

Rotblat concluded his remarks to scientists with the fol-lowing appeal: "At a time when science plays such a powerful role in the life of society, when the destiny of the whole of mankind may hinge on the results of scientific research, it is incumbent on all scientists to be fully conscious of that role, and conduct themselves accordingly. I appeal to my fellow scientists to remember their responsibility to humanity."[42]

In the final words of his Nobel Lecture, he spoke as an elder statesman of humanity: "The quest for a war-free world has a basic purpose: survival. But if in the process we learn how to achieve it by love rather than fear, by kindness rather than by compulsion; if in the process we learn to combine the essential with the enjoyable, the expedient with the benevolent, the practical with the beautiful, this will be an extra incentive to embark on this great task. Above all, remember your humanity."[43]

Men of Conscience

I have discussed the manner in which three important scientists reacted to nuclear weapons production and use. There have been many other scientists—including Linus Pauling, Eugene Rabinowitch and Andrei Sakharov—who have joined in publicly seeking to free the world from the dangers of nuclear arms. But there have also been many scientists who have supported the nuclear arms race and have continued to work on designing and improving nuclear weapons.

Einstein, Szilard and Rotblat believed that nuclear weapons threaten the future of humanity and must be brought under international control and abolished. They sought to eliminate not only nuclear weapons, but war as a human institution. They all contributed to the creation of nuclear weapons, driven by the threat of a potential Nazi-produced atomic weapon, but they all regretted their part and sought to change the course of history. They believed that scientists have an important role to play in educating the general population about nuclear threats and encouraging the public and political leaders to support effective nuclear disarmament, with the goal of returning to a world free of nuclear weapons.

These men have become historical figures because they were men of conscience and courage. They understood that nuclear weapons cast a dark shadow across the human future. They stood not with the power establishments of their day, but with humanity. They are important role models for young scientists and engineers. Their lives and their words convey a crucial message for scientists of today: Contribute your talents constructively to humanity, but withhold them from making and improving armaments, in particular nuclear arms.

The atomic scientists were instrumental in initiating many institutions that continue to work for a nuclear weapon-free world. These include Council for a Livable World; Pugwash Conferences on Science and World Affairs; Federation of American Scientists; and the publication *Bulletin of the Atomic Scientists*. To these can be added newer organizations committed to science for social responsibility, such as Science for Peace in the UK; and the International Network of Engineers and Scientists for Global Responsibility.

As the scientists directly connected with the World War II US Manhattan Project and the British MAUD Committee have passed on, moral responsibilities have fallen to a new generation of scientists. It remains to be seen, though, whether this new generation of scientists will have the passion and persistence to carry on effectively in fighting for a world free of nuclear weapons.

The University of California has managed and provided oversight to the US nuclear weapons laboratory at Los Alamos since 1945 and to the Lawrence Livermore National Laboratory since 1952. These laboratories have designed every nuclear weapon in the US arsenal. The University of California lends its prestige and legitimacy to the development and maintenance of the US nuclear weapons arsenal. Leaders of the University proudly proclaim that they perform a national service, and seem to give little thought to the global nuclear nightmare they are perpetuating.[44]

Scientists everywhere should join together, in the spirit of the Russell-Einstein Manifesto, to speak out and demand that universities, such as the University of California, stop supporting the design, development, testing and manufacture of any weapon of mass destruction, most of all nuclear weapons. They should bring collective pressure to bear upon those scientists who choose to participate in such work. In short, they should follow in the footsteps of Einstein, Szilard and Rotblat, and accept personal and professional responsibility for seeking an end to the nuclear weapons threat to humanity.

As Nagasaki Mayor Tomihisa Taue pointed out in an annual Nagasaki Peace Declaration, "[A] major force for nuclear abolition would be for scientists and engineers to refuse to cooperate in nuclear weapons development."[45] To achieve this end, it will be necessary to apply peer pressure within the scientific community to strip away any semblance of prestige and legitimacy that remains connected to the creation of weapons capable of destroying humanity.

EINSTEIN'S REGRET

Einstein's regret ran deep
Like the pools of sorrow
That were his eyes.

His mind could see things
That others could not,
The bending of light,

The slowing of time,
Relationships of trains passing
In the night, and power,

Dormant and asleep,
That could be awakened,
But who would dare?

He saw patterns
In snowflakes and stars,
Unimaginable simplicity.

When the shadow of Hitler
Spread across Europe
What was Einstein to do?

His regret ran deep, deeper
Than the pools of sorrow
That were his eyes.

Atmospheric Nuclear Testing

The US conducted the first test of a nuclear device in the New Mexico desert on July 16, 1945. The next two uses of nuclear weapons were the bombs dropped on Hiroshima and Nagasaki. In a sense, these could also be considered tests. The first bomb dropped on Hiroshima was a uranium bomb, considered so easy to use that it was not tested beforehand. The bomb dropped on Nagasaki was a plutonium bomb of the type that had been tested at Alamogordo, New Mexico. The bombs dropped on Hiroshima and Nagasaki were tests on two live and captive populations. The results were shown by calculating how many of the test participants were no longer alive at the end of the tests.

Beginning in 1946, the US engaged in a nuclear arms race with itself. It chose the Marshall Islands, a territory entrusted to it by the United Nations Trusteeship Council, for its initial post-war testing. The solo US arms race lasted only until 1949 when the Soviets tested their first nuclear weapon. In 1952, the US tested its first thermonuclear weapon, and a year later the Soviets tested theirs. A serious arms race was in progress, a quantitative race to develop more nuclear weapons, and a qualitative race to develop more powerful nuclear weapons and more accurate delivery systems.

Between 1946 and 1958, the US conducted 67 atmospheric and underwater nuclear tests in the Marshall Islands, the equivalent power of dropping 1.6 Hiroshima bombs each day over the 12-year period. The Marshall Islanders were the guinea pigs for these experiments. They were moved from island to island, and were frequently subjected to radiation from the tests. Many island women reported miscarriages, stillbirths, and live births of babies with extreme deformities, some of whom they described as "jellyfish babies."[46]

The US also tested nuclear weapons at its Nevada Test Site. From 1951 to 1992, when a moratorium on nuclear testing went into effect, the US tested 928 nuclear weapons at the Nevada Test Site. Of these, 828 were underground and 100 above ground. It conducted 126 tests elsewhere, including its tests in the Marshall Islands. In total, above ground and underground, the US conducted 1,054 nuclear tests.[47]

The US, like the other nuclear weapon states, conducted its tests on the lands of indigenous peoples. The Soviets tested at its Semipalatinsk Test Site in Kazakhstan and at Novaya Zemla. It was at the latter site that the Soviets conducted a 50 megaton test, the largest nuclear test ever. The French tested at the Mururoa and Fangatau Atolls in French Polynesia and in the Sahara Desert in Algeria. The British tested on aboriginal lands at Maralinga in South Australia. The Chinese tested at their Lop Nur Test Site in Tibet. The Indians tested at Pokharan in the Rajasthan Desert, the Pakistanis at Chagai Hills in Baluchistan, and the North Koreans at P'uggye-yok.

In total, more than 2,000 nuclear tests have been conducted since the beginning of the Nuclear Age. Of these, over 500 were above ground nuclear tests that spread radiation in the atmosphere and are undoubtedly responsible for the onset of cancers and leukemia in tens of thousands of people throughout the world. The purposes for the tests were in part technological, and in part were to demonstrate a country's prowess, like a boy at the beach flexing his muscles. Helen Caldicott, an Australian pediatrician and leader in the anti-nuclear movement, referred to the psychological dimension of the nuclear arms race with its weapons and missile testing as "missile envy."[48] Insecure leaders demonstrated their country's prowess with big explosions and sleek metallic missiles.

WHEN THE BOMB BECAME OUR GOD

When the bomb became our god
We loved it far too much,
Worshipping no other gods before it.

We thought ourselves great
And powerful, creators of worlds.

We turned toward infinity,
Giving the bomb our very souls.

We looked to it for comfort,
To its smooth metallic grace.

When the bomb became our god
We lived in a constant state of war
That we called *peace.*

The Cuban Missile Crisis

In October 1962, the US and USSR came close to a nuclear exchange over the USSR's placement of nuclear weapons in Cuba. It was a sobering experience for the world when, for 13 days, the US and the USSR stood at the brink of nuclear war. In the end, a deal was struck and the Soviet Union withdrew its missiles and warheads from Cuba in exchange for the US withdrawing its missiles and warheads from Turkey, a *quid pro quo* that President Kennedy insisted be kept secret.[49] When the crisis was over, people throughout the world breathed a sigh of relief. There was widespread, but perhaps not sufficient, recognition of how close the world had come to stumbling over the brink into the abyss of nuclear war.

Later, when many of the principal decision makers in the crisis met and talked about what they had understood and experienced, it became evident that the decision makers were operating on false assumptions, some of which might have triggered nuclear war. The consensus was that they and their countries had been most fortunate to have avoided a devastating nuclear exchange.

DUCK AND COVER

circa 1950

Children,
this is the way you will be saved
from a nuclear attack. At the sound
of the bell you will scramble as fast
as you can under your desk.
Face downward toward the floor
in a kneeling position
with your head resting on your arms.
Keep your eyes squeezed
tightly closed, not opening them
or looking up until you hear me say
"All clear."

This is the way you will be saved
from shards of glass and other objects
traveling at speeds of hundreds of miles
per hour. And from the flash of white
light that could melt your eyeballs. And
from the explosion that could scramble
your brains and the rest of your organs.
And this is the way you will be saved
from the fire that may incinerate you,
leaving you shriveled, charred
and lifeless.

continued

This is the way you will be saved
from the radiation that will cause your gums
to bleed, your hair to fall out, leukemia
to form in your blood, and lead
to either a slow and painful death,
or one more rapid and painful.
Pay close attention to the directions
so that you will get it right the first time.

Banning Atmospheric
Nuclear Testing

Throughout the 1950s, scientists sounded the alarm on atmospheric nuclear testing. They were concerned about the effects of the release of radiation on human health. One of the leaders of this movement was the great scientist Linus Pauling. Together with his wife, Ava Helen, Pauling organized a petition of scientists worldwide to stop the testing. Their effort was a great success, leading to obtaining over 10,000 signatures on their petition. Pauling was called before a Congressional Committee and asked which countries gave him the funding for the project. He replied truthfully that no country had provided funding. The relatively inexpensive petition drive was funded entirely by him and his wife.[50]

In 1963, the US, UK and USSR signed the Partial Test Ban Treaty, agreeing to refrain from nuclear testing in the atmosphere, outer space and under water. The treaty was an important step forward, but it did not stop nuclear testing; it simply moved it underground for its signatories. China and France did not sign the treaty and would continue conducting atmospheric nuclear weapons tests until the 1990s.

The Partial Test Ban Treaty called for speedy negotiations for a Comprehensive Nuclear Test Ban Treaty (CTBT). It would take another 33 years, however, before this treaty would be completed and opened for signatures in 1996. The CTBT, signed now by over 180 countries, still has not entered into force. Since 1992, however, the US and Russia have agreed to a moratorium on underground nuclear testing, and have relied instead on "subcritical" nuclear tests (which are tests that purposefully do not produce a critical mass of fissile material).and computer simulations. They have found ways to continue to test, and thereby improve their nuclear weapons, without reaching criticality in nuclear reactions.

Preventing Proliferation

Beginning in the early 1960s, a serious problem was added to the agendas of the three initial nuclear weapon states, the US, USSR and UK – the problem of nuclear weapons proliferation to other countries. They recognized the dangers of a world with many nuclear weapon states and wanted to contain the spread of nuclear weapons. In the early 1960s, both France and China tested nuclear weapons, bringing the total number of nuclear weapon states at the time to five.

In 1968, the Nuclear Non-Proliferation Treaty (NPT) was opened for signatures. The treaty required non-nuclear weapon states not to develop or otherwise acquire nuclear weapons, but the non-nuclear weapon states negotiated for something in return. They were not prepared to live indefinitely in a two-tier structure of nuclear "haves" and "have-nots." The nuclear "haves" were defined in the treaty as those countries that had exploded a nuclear device prior to January 1, 1967. These countries were: the US, USSR, UK, France and China. All other countries would be considered non-nuclear weapon states. This was the two-tier structure envisioned by the US, USSR and UK.

The treaty called in Article VI for an end to the nuclear arms race at an early date, for good faith negotiations for nuclear disarmament and for general and complete disarmament. For the first time in the Nuclear Age, the nuclear weapon states had put themselves on record agreeing to pursue good faith negotiations to eliminate their nuclear arsenals. However, in the years to follow there would be many countries and leaders who would question, quite appropriately, the good faith of the nuclear weapons states.

The NPT contained a provision in Article IV declaring the peaceful uses of nuclear energy an "inalienable right." It called for the exchange of equipment, materials and technological information for peaceful uses of nuclear energy. The treaty tried, in other words, to promote the "peaceful" atom, while confining its warlike uses to a small number of nuclear weapon states. In doing so, it opened a Pandora's Box. Nuclear energy and research programs would create and use nuclear materials that could be employed in building nuclear weapons.

The treaty called for a conference of its parties to take place 25 years after it entered into force to determine whether the treaty should be extended indefinitely or for a period or periods of time. Since the treaty entered into force in 1970, this conference took place in 1995, the 50th anniversary year of the Hiroshima and Nagasaki bombings. When the parties assembled at the United Nations headquarters in New York, the nuclear weapon states lobbied strongly for the indefinite extension of the treaty, while some of the non-nuclear weapon states argued that such an extension would give a blank check to the nuclear weapon states to continue to evade their nuclear disarmament obligations under the treaty.

In the end, the nuclear weapon states and their allies prevailed and the treaty was extended indefinitely. This led many of the civil society organizations in attendance, which had lobbied against an indefinite extension, to band together and form the Abolition 2000 Global Network. This Network sought the initiation of negotiations by the turn of the millennium for the unconditional elimination of all nuclear weapons. It sought an end to the continuing dangers that nuclear weapons pose to humanity. The Abolition 2000 Founding Statement remains one of the most important declarations of civil society on the need to abolish nuclear weapons. It is shown in Appendix D.

Israel, India and Pakistan

The Non-Proliferation Treaty established a norm against nuclear weapons proliferation, but it also promoted nuclear energy. Behind the cover of "peaceful" nuclear programs, Israel, India and Pakistan all proceeded to develop nuclear weapons. These three countries never joined the NPT, and thus were not bound by its provisions against proliferation, demonstrating the limitations of the existing international legal system.

Israel is thought to have developed its first nuclear weapons in 1967. It has never admitted to having the weapons, but its leaders have responded, when pressed, with the ambiguous statement that Israel will not be the first to introduce nuclear weapons into the Middle East. In 1986, an Israeli nuclear technician, Mordechai Vanunu, released information about Israel's nuclear program to *The Sunday Times* in London. Vanunu was lured to Rome by a female agent of Mossad, the Israeli intelligence agency, where he was kidnapped and taken back to Israel for a secret trial. He was sentenced to 18 years in prison. More than 11 of those years were served in solitary confinement. After serving his 18 years, Vanunu was released from prison, but not allowed to leave Israel or speak with foreign reporters.[51] Israel is thought to possess between 100 and 200 nuclear weapons and is capable of delivering these by bomber aircraft, or land-based or submarine-based ballistic missiles.

India first tested a nuclear device in 1974, claiming the test was for peaceful purposes only. On many occasions, Indian leaders said that they would not develop nuclear weapons if the countries with nuclear weapons would fulfill their obligations under the NPT to disarm their nuclear arsenals. In 1998, three years after the NPT was extended indefinitely, the Indians conducted a series of nuclear tests, demonstrating to the world that they are a nuclear power.

Almost immediately following the Indian tests, the Pakistanis conducted their own set of nuclear tests. India and Pakistan have engaged in a long conflict over Kashmir, on occasion erupting into war. Now both countries possessed nuclear arsenals and the people of India and Pakistan showed their jubilation in the streets. In reality, though, the people of both countries have become hostages to the threat of nuclear Armageddon. Computer models of a nuclear war on the subcontinent show the potential for two billion deaths worldwide from blast, fire, radiation, climate change, crop failure and nuclear famine. South Asia is one of the most dangerous places on the planet.[52]

Nuclear Deterrence

Very few policy makers view nuclear weapons as simply another tool of war, which perhaps explains the extraordinary good fortune of precluding their use in warfare since Hiroshima and Nagasaki. In general, nuclear weapons are viewed as a deterrent to nuclear attack. The weapons themselves, however, cannot provide a country with protection. They are not a shield, but the modern day equivalent of a spear. They cannot be used against another nuclear weapon state, though, without risking a response which would leave the attacking country in ruins. The weapons are justified as being a deterrent force. But nuclear deterrence is a theory of human behavior, and its predictive capability is subject to error with possibly catastrophic consequences.

Nuclear deterrence will not work against a leader who does not believe the threat of retaliation will be carried out, and this is always subject to question. In addition, the potential attacker must act rationally. It is difficult to believe that all leaders will act rationally at all times, particularly under conditions of high stress as in war. Humanity is betting the future of civilization and the human species on the rationality of leaders of the nuclear weapon states.

Also, in tense circumstances, there is pressure on decision makers to consider striking first, thereby seeking to destroy the other side's nuclear arsenal on the ground, before it can be launched. Of course, an attacking country must be concerned that if it fails to destroy all or most of the other side's arsenal, it will likely itself be destroyed in a counterattack. The possibility of a first-strike attack is always present with nuclear arsenals. If the potential victim has nuclear weapons, the potential attacker must exercise care. But if the potential victim does not have nuclear weapons, the potential attacker must exercise self-restraint. It has been the situation in the world since the US atomic bombings of Hiroshima and Nagasaki that nuclear-armed nations and leaders have used restraint, what some call a "nuclear taboo."

Nuclear weapon states have not necessarily been stopped from using nuclear weapons by nuclear deterrence. In actuality, it cannot be proved whether nuclear deterrence has worked or not. We do know that the world has come close to a nuclear exchange on a number of occasions. It makes no sense to bet the future of one's country and of civilization on the effectiveness of nuclear deterrence.

If a country truly believed that nuclear deterrence were effective, it would be unnecessary for it to develop missile defenses. Such defenses are, in effect, an admission that nuclear deterrence is insufficient to prevent nuclear attacks. Missile defenses seek to provide actual physical protection against a nuclear attack rather than only the psychological "protection" of nuclear deterrence. The problem with missile defenses is that they are not reliable and cannot be counted on to stop an attack involving maneuverable nuclear warheads or one using decoys.

An interesting question to consider is: Which country would benefit more from nuclear deterrence, a strong one or a weak one? Let us take the US as an example of a strong country. With all its thousands of nuclear weapons, it cannot deter a terrorist organization in possession of one or more nuclear devices. Terrorists are not likely to be deterred because they cannot be located and they are often suicidal. You cannot deter a group that you cannot locate, since there is no place to threaten with retaliation. Nor can you deter those who are suicidal because they are not threatened by death. Thus, a terrorist organization with nuclear weapons would be the US's worst nightmare. Since it cannot use nuclear deterrence against such an organization, it must, with absolute certainty, prevent nuclear weapons or the materials to make them from falling into the hands of a terrorist organization. The obvious solution to a terrorist nuclear threat is to reduce the number of nuclear weapons and weapons-grade nuclear materials in the world to zero, or to as low an amount as possible, an amount that can be easily monitored and controlled. But the longer the US continues to rely upon nuclear weapons and drag its feet on serious nuclear disarmament, the more likely it is that nuclear weapons will proliferate to other countries and to terrorist groups.

What about a weak country in possession of nuclear weapons? Let us take the case of North Korea. It was a party to the Non-Proliferation Treaty. Its leaders watched President George W. Bush name it as a part of the Axis of Evil. It watched Iraq, another country so named that did not possess nuclear weapons, be attacked, invaded and occupied by the US. In 2006, three years after Iraq was invaded, North Korea tested its first nuclear weapon. Its message to the US was that the US would not be able to do to North Korea what it had done to Iraq. In this sense, nuclear weapons may be thought of as military equalizers. Of course, they do not really put a powerful country and a weak country on an equal footing, but nuclear weapons in the hands of a weak country do put a more powerful country on notice that there would be a heavy price to pay for attacking it with conventional or nuclear weapons.

However, nuclear deterrence can fail for a weak country just as it can fail for a strong country. Nuclear deterrence operates at the psychological level, where miscommunications, misunderstandings, false assumptions and miscalculations can lead to failure. In other words, nuclear deterrence cannot be relied upon to protect a country from attack, nuclear or conventional. It is a dangerous game of chicken that can take both weak and powerful countries over the precipice into nuclear disaster, as nearly happened with the Cuban Missile Crisis in 1962. Those who believe in nuclear deterrence and promote it are indirectly promoting nuclear proliferation and increasing the odds that nuclear weapons will end up in the hands of terrorists who cannot be deterred.

Nuclear Detonation:
Fifteen Scenarios

Many people are ignorant or complacent about nuclear weapons. They deny the nuclear threat and put nuclear dangers out of their minds. This is a dangerous response to a serious threat to humanity. There are many ways in which a nuclear detonation could take place, including by accident, miscalculation or intentional use. Any use of nuclear weapons, including by accident or miscalculation, could lead to the destruction of a city, as occurred at Hiroshima and Nagasaki. Further, a nuclear weapon detonation could trigger a retaliatory response leading to nuclear war and even broader devastation, including the annihilation of complex life on the planet. Listed below are 15 possible scenarios for a nuclear detonation. These are 15 arguments against complacency and for engagement in seeking a world without nuclear weapons.

1. **False Alarm**: A false alarm, which could be set off by a cyber-attacker, triggers a decision to launch a nuclear attack. A false alarm could also be triggered by faulty equipment or by human error.

2. **Unauthorized Launch**: Launch codes are obtained by hackers, espionage agents or by coercion and used to launch high alert forces. This could involve the physical takeover of a mobile missile, or the use of codes obtained via pre-delegation.

3. **Accidental Nuclear War**: An accidental launch leads to an escalation into a nuclear war.

4. **Control and Communications Failure**: A rogue field commander or submarine commander falls out of communication or deliberately puts himself out of communication with his central command and launches a nuclear attack on his own authority.

5. **"Dr. Strangelove" Nuclear War**: The launch of a nuclear attack by a rogue field or submarine commander leads to a retaliatory strike that escalates into a nuclear war.

6. **Terrorist Bomb**: A terrorist group obtains nuclear materials and creates an unsophisticated nuclear device or obtains a bomb and succeeds in detonating it in a city.

7. **Terrorist Bomb Triggers Nuclear War**: A terrorist nuclear attack is disguised in such a way as to appear to come from another nuclear weapon state, leading to a "retaliatory strike" that escalates into nuclear war.

8. **Preemptive Attack**: Believing one's country to be under nuclear attack or about to be under such attack, a leader of a nuclear weapon state launches a preemptive nuclear attack.

9. **Preventive Nuclear War**: A nuclear weapon state launches an unprovoked nuclear attack against another country perceived to pose a future threat. An example would be the use by Israel of small tactical nuclear weapons against deeply buried nuclear facilities in Iran.

10. **Escalation of Conventional War**: India and Pakistan, for example, continue to engage periodically in conventional war over Kashmir. The conflict escalates into a nuclear exchange of approximately 100 Hiroshima-sized nuclear weapons, resulting in nuclear famine and a massive number of deaths.

11. **Military Parity**: In a conventional war, Russia moves to nuclear weapons due to its deteriorating conventional military capability.

12. **Irrational Leader**: An unstable and paranoid leader, fearing attack and/or regime change, launches a nuclear attack against perceived adversaries. There are no democratic controls.

13. **Rational Leader**: A leader, making what he deems to be rational calculations, launches a nuclear attack against perceived adversaries to assure the survival of his country. There are no democratic controls.

14. **Prompt Global Strike**: The US proceeds with plans to place conventional warheads on some of its intercontinental ballistic missiles. One of these missiles, when launched, is mistaken for a nuclear-armed warhead, resulting in a retaliatory nuclear attack.

15. **Intentional Nuclear War**: Tensions and conflict between major nuclear powers mount, leading to an intentional nuclear war. Civilization is destroyed and complex life on Earth is ended. Game over.

Perfection Is a Hard Target

On August 30, 2007, six nuclear-tipped cruise missiles were loaded, by mistake, onto the wings of a B-52 aircraft and flown from Minot Air Force Base in North Dakota to Barksdale Air Force Base in Louisiana. It was a major error in the handling of nuclear weapons, which led to various investigations and the replacement of the commander of Minot Air Force Base. The new commander, Colonel Joel Westa, commented, "Our goal in this line of work is not to make errors—our goal is perfection. It's one of those missions where the tolerance is very low for error, in fact, it is zero."[53]

Colonel Westa sounds like a well-meaning individual, but someone should explain to him that humans are prone to errors, not only of judgment but of memory and inadvertence. For example, on the same day that Colonel Westa was professing that there is zero tolerance for error, February 12, 2008, the US Secretary of Defense, surely not purposefully, slipped on ice outside his home and broke his humerus, the bone connecting the shoulder to the elbow. Accidents occur.

Edward Teller, father of the H-Bomb, recognized, "Sooner or later a fool will prove greater than the proof even in a foolproof system."[54] With some 16,000 nuclear weapons in the world and nearly 2,000 of these weapons still on hair-trigger alert, ready to be fired in moments, and with policies of launch-on-warning in effect in the US, Russia and other nuclear-armed countries, there is, regrettably, fertile ground for proving Teller right about the fool proving greater than the proof.

Mikhail Gorbachev, who had his finger on the nuclear button for many years and who, in the mid-1980s, called for the abolition of nuclear weapons, offered sage advice when he stated that "the infinite and uncontrollable fury of nuclear weapons should never be held in the hands of any mere mortal ever again, for any reason."[55]

Perfection is not possible, but it is possible to abolish nuclear weapons. Our choices are to play nuclear roulette with the human future, seeking an impossible standard of perfection for all possessors of nuclear weapons, or to recognize the wisdom in Gorbachev's words and eliminate the overwhelming danger posed by these weapons by eliminating the weapons themselves.

Nuclear Disarmament

Nuclear deterrence is not sufficient to protect against the use of nuclear weapons, nor is it enough to back up nuclear deterrence with a missile defense system that is subject to failure. The best guarantee against the threat or use of nuclear weapons is their abolition. This was part of the intent of the Non-Proliferation Treaty, when it called for "good faith" negotiations to achieve nuclear disarmament.[56] The International Court of Justice clarified this by saying that the obligation is for complete nuclear disarmament in all its aspects.[57] The Non-Proliferation Treaty is a binding international agreement that requires nuclear weapon states that are parties to the treaty to eliminate their nuclear arsenals. This is also in the national security interests of all countries. As previously argued, nuclear weapons cannot provide physical protection and it is questionable whether they can actually deter. Rather than chase a vision of security by dangerous and morally repugnant technological means, new modes of international cooperation are needed, and at the heart of these and driving them is the necessity of implementing total nuclear disarmament.

Nuclear weapons are subject to accidental as well as intentional use. The longer these weapons remain in the military plans of nuclear weapon states, the greater the danger that they will be used by accident or design. A world without nuclear weapons would be a safer world for all humanity, and the elimination of nuclear weapons would be a great gift to all humanity. In addition to the danger of the immensely destructive power of these weapons, there are many other reasons to seek a world free of nuclear weapons. The weapons themselves are instruments of dehumanization. They diminish their possessors as well as their potential victims. Far from adding to the prestige of a country, they make that country an outlaw nation. They are legally and morally reprehensible and economically enormously wasteful. These weapons should not only be taboo; they should stigmatize their possessors as reckless enemies of humanity.

Nuclear zero would be a great victory for humanity. It would free humanity of these soul-destroying weapons of mass annihilation. It would demonstrate that countries can join together for the common good. It would allow us to use our resources more humanely. It would protect the thousands of future generations to whom we owe a sacred duty to pass the world on intact. Never before has humankind faced such a grave existential challenge. It is the challenge of those of us alive in the Nuclear Age to take action to eliminate nuclear weapons before they eliminate us.

US Leadership for Global Nuclear Disarmament

Two former US Ambassadors for nonproliferation and disarmament, Thomas Graham, Jr. and Max Kampelman, wrote, 'The road from the world of today, with thousands of nuclear weapons in national arsenals to a world free of this threat, will not be an easy one to take, but it is clear that US leadership is essential to the journey and there is growing worldwide support for that civilized call to zero."[58] It is indeed a "civilized call."

The Obama administration took a positive step when it ruled out using nuclear weapons against non-nuclear weapon states that are in compliance with the Non-Proliferation Treaty.[59] It could have gone further, though. While the administration surely sees its posture as a useful threat for states not in compliance with the NPT, this is a two-edged sword. Such threats also send a message to the rest of the world that the US still finds nuclear weapons useful and is willing to threaten their use. This continued reliance on nuclear weapons reinforces the current double standard of nuclear "haves" and "have-nots," which in the long run will not hold. Some states may be encouraged, as was North

Korea, to pursue nuclear weapon capabilities in the belief that they can deter an attack by a more powerful adversary.

The nuclear weapons reductions in the New START agreement are modest and leave more than enough capability on each side to destroy civilization, but they are a step forward and they do extend the important verification provisions of the first START agreement. They should be seen as a platform from which to continue the downward movement in the number of nuclear arms to zero. Ultimately, zero is the only safe, secure and stable number of nuclear weapons in the world.

The US has enormous conventional force capability. While this allows the US to reduce its reliance upon nuclear weapons, it also creates problems with Russia in achieving further nuclear reductions. Russia has repeatedly expressed concerns with US missile defense deployments, US unwillingness to curtail space weaponization, and the US Prompt Global Strike program that would entail putting conventional warheads on ICBMs. To get to substantially lower levels of nuclear arms and finally to zero, the US is going to have to meet the concerns of Russia and other countries that it is not simply making the world "safe" for its own conventional weapons superiority.

So-called political "realists," such as former Secretaries of State George Shultz and Henry Kissinger, support the new nuclear posture of the Obama administration. Critics, such as Senators John McCain and Lindsey Graham, are playing nuclear politics with loaded barrels, pursuing outdated nuclear policies that are MAD in all senses, not only policies of Mutual Assured Destruction but policies based upon Mutual Assured Delusions. The US cannot continue to base its security on nuclear weapons without running the risk of massive and catastrophic disaster.

The US administration should be urged to move rapidly to build on the progress it has made to this point. There is no scenario that would justify US use of nuclear weapons again. Nuclear deterrence is unstable and dangerous. It is a hypothesis and it cannot be proven to be effective under all conditions in the future. It came close to failing on various occasions during the Cold War.[60] Nuclear deterrence relies upon rationality, and it remains a dangerous assumption that all leaders will act rationally at all times. The theory of nuclear deterrence is subject to human fallibility, and human fallibility and nuclear weapons are a flammable mixture.

A stronger indication that President Obama is indeed committed to seeking "the peace and security of a world without nuclear weapons" would be a policy of "No First Use" of nuclear weapons, coupled with taking the weapons off hair-trigger alert and continuing to work with the Russians and then other nuclear weapon states on major reductions in arsenals. The US should be leading the way in pursuing a new treaty, a Nuclear Weapons Convention, for the phased, verifiable, irreversible and transparent elimination of nuclear weapons.

Toward a Nuclear
Weapons Convention

The countries of the world have already negotiated treaties to outlaw and ban chemical and biological weapons: a Chemical Weapons Convention[61] and a Biological Weapons Convention,[62] respectively. A new treaty is needed, a Nuclear Weapons Convention, to outlaw and ban nuclear weapons. Such a treaty would also set forth the process by which nuclear weapons are to be eliminated. It would be *phased* to allow for confidence building among nations with each step forward. It would be *verifiable* so that each country could be assured that the steps required were being fulfilled. It would be *irreversible* so that it would not be possible for countries to quickly or easily reinstitute their nuclear weapons programs. Finally, it would be *transparent* so that countries would know where they stand at each step in the process.

The new treaty could build upon Article VI of the Non-Proliferation Treaty, which contains the commitment of the nuclear weapon states to pursue good faith negotiations for nuclear disarmament. The new treaty, when negotiated and completed, would replace the Non-Proliferation Treaty. Without nuclear weapons in the world and with the fissile materials to make these weapons under strict international control, nuclear proliferation would no longer loom as a major problem in the world.

Civil society organizations have prepared a Model Nuclear Weapons Convention, which has been introduced to the United Nations General Assembly by Costa Rica and Malaysia.[63] This Model Convention shows that it is possible to create a treaty that would deal with the technical issues of nuclear weapons abolition. What remains to be seen, though, is whether the political will can be generated to commence negotiations among countries for such a treaty.

It will require leadership to convene the countries of the world to begin the process of negotiating the Nuclear Weapons Convention. It would be appropriate for this leadership to come from the United States, the country that brought us into the Nuclear Age, the only country to have used nuclear weapons in warfare, and the world's most militarily powerful country. But it seems clear that the US is not yet prepared to provide such leadership. If the US does not provide the needed leadership, it can come from other countries, for in fact all countries and all peoples have a vested interest in a nuclear weapon-free future.

Ronald Reagan:
A Nuclear Abolitionist

It is worth reflecting on conservative icon Ronald Reagan's legacy with regard to nuclear weapons. According to his wife, Nancy Reagan, "Ronnie had many hopes for the future, and none were more important to America and to mankind than the effort to create a world free of nuclear weapons."[64]

President Reagan was a nuclear abolitionist. He believed that the only reason to have nuclear weapons was to prevent the then Soviet Union from using theirs. Understanding this, he argued in his 1984 State of the Union address, "A nuclear war cannot be won and must never be fought. The only value in our two nations possessing nuclear weapons is to make sure they will never be used. But then would it not be better to do away with them entirely?"[65]

Ronald Reagan regarded nuclear weapons, according to Nancy, as "totally irrational, totally inhumane, good for nothing but killing, possibly destructive of life on earth and civilization."[66]

In 1986, President Reagan and General Secretary Gorbachev met for a summit in Reykjavik, Iceland. In a remarkable quirk of history, the two men shared a vision of a world free of nuclear weapons. Despite the concerns of their aides, they came close to achieving agreement on this most important of issues. The sticking point was that President Reagan saw his Strategic Defense Initiative (missile defenses) as being essential to the plan, and Gorbachev couldn't accept this (even though Reagan promised to share the US missile defense system with the then Soviet Union). Gorbachev wanted missile defense development to be restricted to the laboratory for ten years. Reagan couldn't accept this.

The two leaders came heartbreakingly close to ending the era of nuclear weapons, but in the end they couldn't achieve their mutual goal. As a result, nuclear weapons have proliferated and remain a danger to all humanity. Today, we face the threat of terrorists gaining possession of nuclear weapons, and wreaking massive destruction on the cities of powerful nations. There can be no doubt that had Reagan and Gorbachev succeeded, the US and the world would be much safer, and these men would be remembered, above all else, for this achievement.

The *USS Ronald Reagan* has the motto, "Peace through Strength." President Reagan was known for his commitment to this motto, but he never saw nuclear weapons as a strength. In his book, *Ronald Reagan and His Quest to Abolish Nuclear Weapons,* Paul Lettow quotes Reagan as saying, "I know that there are a great many people who are pointing to the unimaginable horror of nuclear war.... [T]o those who protest against nuclear war, I can only say, 'I'm with you.'"[67] Lettow also quotes Reagan as stating, "[M]y dream is to see the day when nuclear weapons will be banished from the face of the Earth."[68]

In the 18th and 19th centuries, individuals struggled to achieve the abolition of slavery because they understood that every man, woman and child has the right to live in freedom. Through the efforts and persistence of committed individuals like William Wilberforce in Great Britain and Frederick Douglass in the United States, slavery was brought to an end, and humanity is better for it. In today's world, we confront an issue of even greater transcending importance, because nuclear weapons place civilization and the human species itself in danger of annihilation.

Ronald Reagan, a staunch conservative, was a leader who recognized this and worked during his presidency for the abolition of these inhumane weapons. He believed, according to Nancy, that "as long as such weapons were around, sooner or later they would be used," with catastrophic results.[69] He understood that nuclear weapons themselves are the enemy.

Unfortunately, Ronald Reagan died before seeing his goal of abolishing nuclear weapons realized. It is up to those of us still living to complete this job. It is not a partisan issue, but rather a human issue, one that affects our common future.

Changing the Climate
of Complacency

There is a strong need to change the climate of our thinking, specifically the passive acceptance of the abuse of our planet and its myriad species, including our own. In this sense, humanity lives far too much in a "climate" of ignorance and indifference. We have organized ourselves into consumer societies that demonstrate little concern for our responsibilities to the planet, to each other and to the future.

There are many ongoing problems in the world that deserve our awareness and engagement. The fact that these problems receive insufficient attention and action speaks to the sea change that is needed. Many of these problems were identified in the eight United Nations Millennium Development Goals: eradicating extreme poverty and hunger; achieving universal primary education; promoting gender equality; reducing child mortality; reducing maternal mortality; combating HIV/AIDS, malaria and other diseases; ensuring environmental sustainability; and establishing a global partnership for development.[70]

While these major problems on our planet are not adequately addressed, the world's countries are spending more than $1.7 trillion annually on their military establishments. Many states are attempting to create military security at the expense of human security. The poor on the planet are being marginalized while rich countries use their scientific resources and material wealth to produce ever more deadly and destructive armaments. In a climate of complacency, the military-industrial complexes of the world overindulge their gluttonous appetites while the poor and politically powerless of the Earth are left to suffer and die.[71]

At the apex of the global order, the countries that emerged victorious in World War II anointed themselves as permanent members of the United Nations Security Council. They continue to flaunt international law by their reliance upon nuclear weapons and by failing to engage in good faith negotiations for the elimination of these weapons as required by the Non-Proliferation Treaty.

If the world continues on its present path, an increasing number of nations will seek to protect themselves with nuclear weapons (an impossibility), the threat of nuclear annihilation and climate change will continue to hang over our collective heads, extreme poverty in its many manifestations will persist, and we will follow either a slow path to extinction or a rapid one.

This is why we must change the climate of indifference and complacency that currently prevails upon our planet. We humans have the gifts of consciousness and conscience, but these gifts must be used in order to be effective. We must become conscious of what threatens our common future and we must care enough to demand that these threats be eliminated. The only force powerful enough to challenge the corporate and military power that has led us to the precipice is the power of an engaged global citizenry. This remains the one truly great superpower on Earth, but it can only be activated by compassion and caring.

If we do not care enough about the future to engage in the fight to save our planet from catastrophe and our species from omnicide, we need only continue our complacency and leave the important decisions about protecting the environment and human life to powerful corporations and the world's militaries. They have a plan, one based upon dangerous technologies and plunder. Their plan is short-sighted, designed to further enrich the already overly rich. To be silent is, in effect, to vote for their plan.

As Albert Camus, the great French author and existentialist, wrote in the immediate aftermath of the Hiroshima bombing: "Our technical civilization has just reached its greatest level of savagery. We will have to choose, in the more or less near future, between collective suicide and the intelligent use of our scientific conquests.... Before the terrifying prospects now available to humanity, we see even more clearly that peace is the only battle worth waging. This is no longer a prayer but a demand to be made by all peoples to their governments—a demand to choose definitively between hell and reason."[72]

Let us stand with Camus in waging peace. Let us stand with Camus in choosing reason. Let us raise our voices and choose peace and a human future. Let us fulfill the responsibility of each generation to pass the world on intact to the next generation. We are the first generations that have faced the choice of silence and annihilation, or engagement and rebuilding the paradise of our precious planet—the only one we know of in the universe that supports life.

From Complacency
to Compassion

To be complacent in the face of the existential threat to humanity posed by nuclear weapons is to fail the most important test of the Nuclear Age. In 1996, in the aftermath of the end of the Cold War and the breakup of the Soviet Union, Ukraine gave up its inherited nuclear arsenal and sent the weapons to Russia for dismantlement. When its last nuclear weapon had been sent to Russia, there was a ceremony held at a former Ukrainian missile base that once threatened the United States with its long-range nuclear-armed missiles. The Defense Ministers of Ukraine and Russia were joined by the US Secretary of Defense, William Perry. The three defense officials planted sunflowers where the missiles had once been. Secretary Perry said, "Sunflowers instead of missiles in the soil will ensure peace for future generations."[73]

It is hard to imagine defense officials presiding over a ceremony to replace missiles with sunflowers, but it happened and it was a great example of compassion in action. The manmade metallic missiles, conveyers of death, were replaced with sunflowers, regenerating gifts of life. Instruments of mass annihilation were replaced with flowers that turn toward the sun and produce nutritious seeds. There could be no starker contrast than nuclear-armed missiles and sunflowers. One produces terror; the other, natural beauty and health. The ceremony at the Ukrainian missile base is a model for the world.

Sadako Sasaki was two years old when the atomic bomb exploded over Hiroshima. She was a healthy and happy child. She grew into a bright and lively young girl and a fast runner. When she was 12, though, she developed leukemia, a disease associated with radiation exposure. There is a Japanese legend that one's wish will be granted upon folding 1,000 paper cranes. Sadako folded paper cranes in her hospital bed in the hope that she would fulfill her wish for peace and to be healthy again. She wrote, "I will write peace on your wings, and you will fly all over the world." Sadako folded 1,000 paper cranes and continued to fold more. Although she died without her wish for her health being fulfilled, her story and her courage inspired people throughout Japan and throughout the world. Today, children around the world fold paper cranes in honor of Sadako and her wish for peace. In the Hiroshima Peace Memorial Park there is a statue of Sadako that is always surrounded by colorful paper cranes. These cranes, powered by the hearts of children, truly fly peace all over the world.

Nuclear weapons challenge our humanity. We cannot continue indefinitely to live in a nuclear-armed world without significant risk of the weapons being used by accident or design. We tempt fate and put at risk our existence as a species. We threaten our own children. At one time we dealt with these threats by teaching children to fall under their desks in "duck and cover" drills. Which do we prefer for our children: A world of nuclear-armed missiles or a world of sunflowers? A world in which nuclear annihilation is poised to fly on missiles and bombers, or a world where peace flies on the wings of paper cranes? We must choose. We must use our great human gifts of conscience and imagination, and choose wisely. Complacency is a choice, but the future calls to us to take the leap from complacency to compassion.

SADAKO AND THE SHAKUHACHI

We remember Hiroshima not for the past, but for the future. We remember Hiroshima so that its past will not become our future. Hiroshima is best remembered with the plaintive sounds of the bamboo flute, the shakuhachi. It conjures up the devastation, the destruction, the encompassing emptiness of that day. The shakuhachi reveals the tear in the fabric of humanity that was ripped open by the bomb.

Nuclear weapons are not weapons at all. They are a symbol of an imploding human spirit. They are a fire that consumes the air of decency. They are a crossroads where science joined hands with evil and apathy. They are a triumph of academic certainty wrapped in the convoluted lie of nuclear deterrence. They are Einstein's regret. They are many things, but not weapons—not instruments of war, but of genocide and perhaps of omnicide.

Those who gather to retell and listen to the story of Hiroshima and of Sadako are a community, a community committed to a human future. We may not know one another, but we are a community. And we are part of a greater community gathered throughout the world to commemorate the anniversary of the bombing, seeking to turn Hiroshima to Hope.

If we succeed, Sadako of a thousand cranes will be remembered by new generations. She will be remembered long after the names and spirits of those who made and used the bomb will have faded into the haunting sounds of the shakuhachi.

A Dialogue between Einstein and Socrates

Socrates was taking a walk through the countryside and he came across Professor Einstein. After the two men greeted each other, Socrates asked Einstein about his famous quotation concerning the atomic bomb: *"The unleashed power of the atom has changed everything save our modes of thinking, and thus we drift toward unparalleled catastrophe."*

Socrates: I've often wondered about this statement. What exactly did you mean by "modes of thinking"?

Einstein: I meant that the new weapons we have created require us to think in a new way. We can no longer continue to use our old ways of thinking that have brought us this far. Our thinking must change.

Socrates: How must it change?

Einstein: To start with, we must recognize that these weapons have the power to destroy everything, including most life on the planet. We must make greater use of our imaginations, and imagine the outcome of a nuclear war. We must be able to imagine the outcome of a war that would end civilization and cause the death of all humans.

Socrates: This may be difficult for many people to imagine.

Einstein: I have no doubt that it is difficult to imagine because we tend to project the past into the future, but in the Nuclear Age the future could be very different from the past. A future without human life, or even all life, is easier to imagine than it will be to prevent from occurring.

Socrates: You mean imagining a future without a human presence on the planet is the easier part of changing our modes of thinking?

Einstein: Exactly so, Socrates. But it is very important.

Socrates: Why do you find it so important?

Einstein: If you can imagine that we could have a world without human beings, then it should be motivating to do something to prevent this from happening.

Socrates: Yes, Einstein. I can see that this would be motivating. But why aren't more people motivated?

Einstein: First, they aren't motivated because they can't really imagine such a world. Second, even if they can imagine it, they can't figure out what to do.

Socrates: The first problem, the failure of imagination, could be solved with education.

Einstein: Yes, the right kind of education would help greatly.

Socrates: And what would be the right kind of education?

Einstein: Education that shows how devastating the use of these weapons would be. I have always felt that scientists should lead in providing this education, but political leaders should also educate in this regard. And also teachers in classrooms must help educate a new generation.

Socrates: But many people still think that nuclear weapons make them safer.

Einstein: This is an old mode of thinking. It must be changed through education. Nuclear weapons, rather than making us safer, make the world far more dangerous.

Socrates: But many leaders say that the threat to use nuclear weapons prevents other states from using nuclear weapons against you.

Einstein: That, too, is an old mode of thinking. It is called deterrence, and it relies upon the rationality of other leaders. I've always believed in rationality, but I cannot believe that it makes sense to risk the future of humanity on the assumption that all leaders will act rationally at all times and under all circumstances.

Socrates: I can't imagine leaders who are rational all the time.

Einstein: It would be irrational to believe that all leaders are rational at all times.

Socrates: Yes, surely there are times when even the most rational leaders act irrationally. This is true of all humans.

Einstein: Then surely we should not risk the future of the human species due to an unwarranted belief in the nature of rationality.

Socrates: Do you find spirituality to be more important than rationality?

Einstein: I find both are important human capacities requiring further development, and such development requires that we should not put the human species at risk of nuclear annihilation.

Socrates: There is much we can imagine, but also much that is beyond our ability to imagine.

Einstein: Of course, Socrates. But we must expand our capacity to imagine. Nuclear weapons make this necessary.

Socrates: You said that even those who could imagine a world without humans due to nuclear war still may not be able to imagine a way out of the dilemma.

Einstein: Yes, to imagine a world without humans is only a way to understand that we must act to prevent this.

Socrates: But some humans may view a world without humans as a positive outcome.

Einstein: It would mean not only the end of the present and the future—that is bad enough—but also the eradication of all memory of the past, the end of every beautiful thing ever created by humans. There would be no one to appreciate music and poetry, art and architecture, no memory of great or small human triumphs of the past.

Socrates: There would be no one to remember the heroes and heroines of the past.

Einstein: It would be a world without humans. It would destroy the mirror of self-awareness that humans hold up to the universe.

Socrates: That would indeed be a great loss. How can we prevent this from happening?

Einstein: It will require us to summon our creativity and discipline, perhaps more than we have ever done before.

Socrates: This is indeed a great challenge.

Einstein: It is the challenge made necessary by the creation of nuclear weapons.

Socrates: So it is one burst of creativity that brings on the need for new creativity.

Einstein: Exactly so. We need new creative thinking. This problem is solvable. It just needs our best thinking.

Socrates: What do you recommend, Einstein?

Einstein: We must be bold and meet this new danger with a new way of thinking. War can no longer be a way to settle differences between competing powers.

Socrates: So you would do away with war?

Einstein: We must. There is no choice. In a nuclear armed world, war has become too dangerous.

Socrates: Even though I was a soldier and am proud of it, I understand that wars must end. War was never a healthy way to solve conflicts between contending parties.

Einstein: You have a far more positive view of war than I do, but I'm glad we agree that nuclear weapons have made it far too dangerous to continue waging war.

Socrates: For a long time, countries have tried to achieve peace by preparing for war.

Einstein: But this has never worked as they had hoped. Preparing for war has always led to war. Now we must change this paradigm and seek peace by preparing for peace.

Socrates: This makes sense. This is the way forward.

Einstein: There is more. Strong states can no longer prevail in war, as was once the case. With nuclear weapons, even a small extremist group will be able to destroy a powerful country.

Socrates: All the more reason to end war and to do away with nuclear arms.

Einstein: There is no global problem that can any longer be solved without global cooperation. That is also an essential new way of thinking that is necessary for global survival.

Socrates: So we must learn to think as global citizens, owing our allegiance to humanity.

Einstein: I believe this with all my heart. We must also end double standards, and have a single standard that applies to all countries and all people.

Socrates: All of what you say makes sense to me, Einstein, but how can it come to pass?

Einstein: It won't come from our leaders. They are still leading in the old modes of thinking based on arms and force. They still believe in double standards, and the strong countries seek to impose their will on the weak. Leaders of nuclear-armed states won't give up their weapons without being pressed to do so by their people.

Socrates: Then the people must be awakened, and they must demand an end to war, and a world free of nuclear weapons.

Einstein: Yes, Socrates, you are a wise man. You understand the changes in thinking that are necessary.

Socrates: I doubt that I am a wise man, Einstein, but you restore my belief in humanity. I will help you to awaken humanity to the dangers that now confront us and to the need to change our modes of thinking.

Why We Wage Peace

Some things are worth Waging Peace for: our planet and its diverse life forms, including humankind; our children and their dreams; our common future. All of these are threatened by the possibility of nuclear catastrophe.

We live on an amazing planet, the only one we know of in the universe that supports life, and does so in abundance and diversity. Our planet is worth Waging Peace for – against those who are despoiling and ruining its delicate and beautiful environment.

On our unique planet are creatures of all shapes and sizes: birds that fly, fish that swim, animals that inhabit jungles and deserts, mountains and plains, rivers and oceans. Life is worth Waging Peace for – against those who are disrespecting and destroying the habitats of creatures great and small.

Among the diverse creatures on our planet are human beings. We are homo sapiens, the knowing ones, and are relative newcomers to the planet. Yet, our impact has been profound. We are creatures capable of learning and loving, of being imaginative and inventive, of being compassionate and kind. We are worth Waging Peace for – against those who would diminish us by undermining our dignity and human rights.

Human beings, like other forms of life, produce off-spring who are innocent and helpless at birth. All human children require care and nurturing as they grow to maturity. The world's children are worth Waging Peace for – against those who would threaten their future with war and other forms of overt and structural violence.

Children as they grow have dreams of living happy and decent lives, dreams of building a better future in peaceful and just societies. These dreams are worth Waging Peace for—against those whose myopia and greed rob children everywhere of a better future.

Each generation shares a responsibility to pass the planet and civilization on intact to the next generation. Accepting this responsibility is an important part of Waging Peace. It is a way of paying a debt of gratitude to all who have preceded us on the planet by assuring that there is a better future.

In the Nuclear Age, we humans, by our cleverness, have invented tools capable of our own demise. Nuclear weapons are not really weapons; they are instruments of annihilation and perhaps of omnicide, the death of all. Waging Peace in the Nuclear Age requires that we awaken to the threat that these weapons pose to our species and all life, and work to rid the world of these insane tools of global devastation.

For too long humanity has lived with nuclear policies of Mutually Assured Destruction, with the appropriate acronym of MAD. We need a new and distinctly different formulation: Planetary Assured Security and Survival, with the acronym PASS for passing the world on intact to the next generation.

Among the greatest obstacles to assuring survival in the Nuclear Age are ignorance, apathy, complacency and despair. These can only be overcome by education and advocacy; education to raise awareness of what needs to change and advocacy to increase engagement in bringing about the needed change.

The Frog's Malaise

If a frog is dropped into a pot of scalding water, it will immediately jump out. However, if a frog is dropped into a pot of tepid water and the water temperature is gradually raised, the frog will succumb rather than trying to escape.

We humans are like the frog in this story. At the onset of the Nuclear Age we were dropped into a pot of tepid water and here we sit as the temperature of the water rises.

What Keeps the Frog in the Pot?

If the frog continues treading water as the temperature rises, it will eventually die. Why does the frog fail to take action to save itself while the water temperature rises?

If we can ascribe to the frog some human reasoning skills and other human characteristics, the following may be some of the principal factors that explain its failure to act, and also ours.

- **Ignorance**. The frog may fail to recognize the dilemma. It may be unable to predict the consequences of being in water in which the temperature is steadily rising.

- **Complacency**. The frog may feel comfortable in the warming water. It may believe that because nothing bad has happened yet, nothing bad will happen in the future.

- **Deference to Authority**. The frog may believe that others are in control of the thermostat and that decisions of those in authority should be respected.

- **Sense of Powerlessness**. The frog may fail to realize its own power to effect change, and that it has no power to change the conditions in which it finds itself.

- **Fear**. The frog may have concluded that, although there are dangers in the pot, the dangers outside the pot are even greater. Thus, it fails to take action, even though it could do so.

- **Economic Advantage**. The frog may believe, based on cost-benefit analysis, that there are greater short-term rewards for staying in the pot than jumping out.

- **Conformity**. The frog may see other frogs treading water in the pot and not want to appear different by sounding an alarm or acting on its own initiative.

- **Marginalization**. The frog may have witnessed other frogs attempting to raise warnings or jump out, and seen them marginalized and ignored by the other frogs.

- **Technological Optimism**. The frog may understand that there is a problem that could lead to its demise, but believe that it is not necessary to act because someone will find a technological solution.

- **Tyranny of Experts**. Even though the frog may believe it is in danger, the experts may provide a comforting assessment that makes the frog doubt its own wisdom.

Taking the Frog Out of the Pot

Those who put the frog into the pot are not likely to be the same ones to take the frog out. We need new leadership and, as Einstein warned, a new way of thinking. There is only one way out of the nuclear weapons pot, and that is by cooperation on a global scale. Absent such cooperation and the leadership to attain it, further nuclear proliferation and the use of nuclear weapons by accident or design appear inevitable.

Once the water in the pot has heated up, it is doubtful that the frog can get out of the pot by itself. The frog's dilemma can only be resolved by getting it out of the pot or turning down the heat. Resolving the nuclear dilemma confronting humanity will require cooperation—cooperation among people and cooperation among countries. Currently, the nuclear weapon states, led by the United States, are blocking that cooperation. That is why it is essential for US citizens to press their government for leadership in achieving agreement for the phased, verifiable, irreversible and transparent elimination of nuclear weapons in all countries. It is also why the leadership of non-nuclear weapon states calling for effective nuclear disarmament is so important.

The frog needs help getting out of the pot, but this help is unlikely to be forthcoming unless it asks for help. To end the nuclear threat to humanity requires all of us to raise our voices and demand the elimination of nuclear weapons.

The word croak has two meanings. One is the sound of a frog's voice. The other is slang for "to die." By recognizing the frog's malaise and using our voices, we have the capability to prevent the widespread death and destruction that is the predictable result of continuing to base national security on the threat to use nuclear weapons. If we fail to recognize the seriousness of the frog's malaise and our own and fail to act to end the nuclear threat, the result over time will be the demise of us all.

What Nuclear Weapons Teach Us about Ourselves

Nuclear weapons are the most fearsome and destructive killing devices yet created by humankind. They have the capacity to destroy cities, countries and civilization. Yet, although these weapons give rise to some concern and worry, most humans on the planet are complacent about the inherent dangers of these weapons. It is worth exploring what our seeming indifference toward these weapons of mass annihilation teaches us about ourselves, and how we might remedy our malaise.

1. **We are ill-informed.** We appear to go about our daily lives with a self-assured degree of comfort that we will not be affected by the dangers of the weapons. *We need more education about the extreme dangers and risks posed by nuclear weapons.*

2. **We are tribal.** We divide ourselves into national tribes and identify with our own tribe while demonizing "the other." *We need to be more global in our thinking. We need to think as members of the human species, not as members of a national tribe.*

3. **We are self-serving**. We see our own nuclear weapons and/or those of our allies as being positive and useful, while we view the nuclear weapons of our enemies as being negative and harmful. *We need to realize that nuclear weapons, as instruments of indiscriminate mass destruction, are illegal, immoral and dangerous in any hands, including our own.*

4. **We are arrogant**. We seem to take perverse pride in our cleverness at having created such overwhelmingly powerful weapons. *We need to take pride in constructive uses of our science-based technologies, and recognize the inherent dangers and immorality of their destructive uses.*

5. **We are pathological**. We rely for our protection upon these weapons that threaten to kill millions of innocent civilians. *We need to realize that true security cannot be based upon the threat of mass murder of innocent people.*

6. **We are deluded**. We believe that we will not survive threats from "the other" if we do not rely upon these weapons of mass annihilation for our security. *We need to engage "the other" in dialogue until we realize that our common humanity supersedes our differences, and our common future demands our unity.*

7. **We are reckless**. We are willing to bet the human species and the human future that we can keep these weapons under control. *We need to stop playing nuclear roulette with the human future.*

8. **We are foolish**. We trust our leaders to act responsibly, so as to keep nuclear weapons under control. *We*

need to realize that this is too great a responsibility for any person and that all leaders do not act responsibly at all times.

9. **We are timid**. We do not challenge the status quo, which gives rise to such extreme dangers. *We need to confront the challenges posed by nuclear weapons and give voice to our legitimate fears of the weapons themselves.*

10. **We are adolescent**. As a species, we have not matured to the point of taking responsibility for, and directly confronting, the nuclear threat to ourselves and future generations. *We need to grow up and take responsibility to assure our common future for ourselves and generations yet unborn.*

Individually and collectively, we are threatened by nuclear weapons in the arsenals of nine countries. If we fail to act expeditiously to abolish these arsenals, the consequences are likely to be nuclear weapons proliferation to other countries and eventually their use. The question that confronts humanity is: Can we end the Nuclear Age and ensure our survival as a species? To do this, we will need to change our thinking about the weapons and about ourselves. Preventing such catastrophes must begin with changing our thinking, followed by engaging in actions to end the danger. Species-wide threats must be faced with species-wide awareness and engagement.

The further question that awaits an answer, assuming we can change our modes of thinking, is whether we are sufficiently powerful to control and eliminate the threats posed by the weapons. Individually we are not and nationally we are not. But collectively and globally we have the potential to assert a constructive power for change that is far greater than the destructive power of the weapons themselves.

Two *Hibakusha*

At the Nuclear Age Peace Foundation, we have been host to many *hibakusha*, survivors of the atomic bombings. Two who visited the Foundation were Junko Kayashige, who was six years old when the bomb fell on Hiroshima, and Miyako Yano, who was fourteen years old when the bomb fell.

These two *hibakusha*, and all atomic bomb survivors, are ambassadors of the Nuclear Age. Their goals are to rid the world of nuclear weapons and to help humanity move past its age-old penchant for solving conflicts by resorting to war. They understand from personal experience that war in the Nuclear Age is a catalyst for nuclear annihilation.

The women traveled from Hiroshima to the United States to tell their stories in the hope that their past will not become someone else's future. They wish that no one else will suffer the fate of the victims at Hiroshima and Nagasaki. Junko Kayashige stated, "There is not much time left for us *hibakusha*. We must find ways to not create even one more *hibakusha*."

The two women spoke to students at a local college and to assemblies at two high schools. The students paid rapt attention to the personal stories of these witnesses to history. Throughout their lives both women carried the fear that they would be stricken with cancer, leukemia or other radiation-related diseases, the fate of so many victims of the atomic bombings. They also worried that their radiation exposure would affect their children or grandchildren.

Miyako Yano, the older of the two women, was a second year student in a girls' high school when the bomb was dropped. Her class had been assigned the task of helping to clean up the rubble in the city, near to what would become the epicenter of the bombing. On the day of the bombing she was ill and stayed home. By this chance occurrence, her life was saved. If the bombing had occurred the day before, she would have met certain death while working just 500 meters from the epicenter, as was the fate of her classmates the next day. Her family lived four kilometers from the epicenter of the detonation. At this distance, they survived the bomb and helped take care of the injured, many of whom died of radiation poisoning. Miyako was given the task of incinerating the dead.

Junko Kayashige shared a photograph of her family taken just before the bombing. It was a somber picture of a family gathered in wartime. Her older brother was about to go off to war, and the family thought it was the last photograph that would be taken of them all together. It was, in fact, the last photograph of them all together, but for a different reason. Hiroshima suffered the atomic bombing and two of her sisters were victims. Her father was able to find one of his daughters whose back was badly burned, with maggots crawling in the raw wounds. The family tried to help her, but she died ten days later from radiation poisoning. The other sister, who had gone out on an errand, was never found.

Most Americans have an uncomplicated and at best incomplete understanding of the atomic bombings, based on a perspective of the bombings from above; that is, from the perspective of the bombers, rather than from the perspective of the victims. The absence of the victims in the perspective of the victors leaves a large hole that can be filled by the accounts of the survivors of bombed cities. This is necessary not only for a fuller understanding of the past, but for creating a more secure future.

If the world continues upon the path it is on, with a small number of countries relying upon nuclear weapons for their "security," eventually these weapons will be used again, by accident or design. Yesterday's victors may become tomorrow's victims. The United States, the country with the greatest military power the world has ever seen, could be brought to its knees by a terrorist group in possession of nuclear weapons.

There is only one way to end this threat, and that is to abolish these weapons. The *hibakusha* are clear that nuclear weapons and human beings cannot coexist. Either nuclear weapons must be eliminated or human beings face the threat of extinction by weapons of their own creation.

The *hibakusha* continue to warn us of the perils that nuclear weapons pose to the human future. They have long ago forgiven their attackers and speak only from hearts of kindness. Miyako Yano stated, "I believe the A-bombs were dropped not on Hiroshima and Nagasaki alone, but on the entire humanity. We have no choice but to abolish nuclear weapons."

The aging *hibakusha* challenge each of us to act upon their warnings. Their voices are soft but clear. They summon us to achieve the political will to rid the world of this overriding threat.

A Silly Dream?

A note recently came to the Nuclear Age Peace Foundation that said: "Are you folks out of your minds? The nuclear genie is out of the bottle and isn't going back in. Shortly even non-state actors will have nukes! Quit wasting your time on this silly dream." The author of the note, to his credit, signed his name, and also indicated that he is a retired colonel in the US Air Force.

The colonel poses a critical question: Are we out of our minds to believe that change is possible and that humans might find a way to cooperate to eliminate the existential threat that nuclear weapons pose to humanity (and other forms of life)? Perhaps we are, but it seems to me that the future of civilization, the human species and other complex forms of life are worth the effort. The Nuclear Age is distinct from the periods that preceded it in having the technological capacity to end most complex life, including human life, on the planet. The fight for the elimination of nuclear weapons is also the fight for human survival and for the rights of future generations. I've always believed that we have a choice: nuclear weapons or a human future. Along with the survivors of Hiroshima and Nagasaki, I believe it is unlikely that both are possible.

Next, the colonel asserts, "The nuclear genie is out of the bottle and isn't going back in." I suppose this means that the knowledge of how to create nuclear weapons exists and cannot be erased. Granted, the knowledge now exists. The challenge is whether countries will choose to eliminate nuclear weapons in their common interest, or whether they will be paralyzed by fear from trying. Knowledge alone is not sufficient to make nuclear weapons. Scientific and engineering skills are also needed, as are nuclear materials. There may not be a foolproof method to assure the elimination of nuclear weapons, but there is also no foolproof method to assure that existing nuclear weapons will not be used in a nuclear war that would kill hundreds of millions of people and destroy civilization.

The question is: Which is a safer path for humanity? On the one hand, to seek the phased, verifiable, irreversible and transparent elimination of nuclear weapons and effective international safeguards on nuclear materials; or, on the other hand, to continue the status quo of having the world divided into a small but increasing number of nuclear "haves" and a far larger number of nuclear "have-nots"? I would place my bet on working for the elimination of the weapons, the path chosen by Albert Einstein, Mikhail Gorbachev, Ronald Reagan and many others.

The colonel seems to accept the odds of continuing with the status quo, even though he recognizes that "[s]hortly even non-state actors will have nukes!" This is most likely true and it poses an enormous problem for the US and other nuclear-armed countries if we fail to bring nuclear weapons and the materials to make them under strict and effective international control. All of the thousands of nuclear weapons in the US arsenal can't deter a terrorist organization in possession of a single nuclear weapon. You can't credibly threaten retaliation against an organization or individuals that you can't even locate.

"Quit wasting your time," the colonel admonishes, "on this silly dream." But all dreams may seem silly before they are realized. Mahatma Gandhi had a dream of an independent India. It must have seemed silly to Winston Churchill and other British leaders at the time. Martin Luther King, Jr. had a dream of racial equality. Perhaps it seemed silly to many. Nelson Mandela dreamed of an end to apartheid in South Africa. During much of his 27 years in prison, this dream must have seemed silly to the white power structure in South Africa.

There are dreams of justice and equality that must seem silly to many. There are dreams of alleviating poverty and hunger, and dreams of educational opportunity for all children. There are even dreams of eliminating war. It is not silly to fight for a better future, and certainly not silly to fight to assure the future itself.

Each new day brings new hope. We must choose hope and find a way to fight for the dream of peace and the elimination of nuclear weapons. Achieving these goals is the great challenge of our time, and on their success rests the realization of all other goals for a more just and decent world.

Rejecting Nuclear Deterrence

I n 2011, the Nuclear Age Peace Foundation held a conference on "The Dangers of Nuclear Deterrence." This conference focused on the many flaws in nuclear deterrence theory. It concluded by adopting a Santa Barbara Declaration, "Reject Nuclear Deterrence: An Urgent Call to Action." Due to the importance of the Declaration, I include it in full below.

SANTA BARBARA DECLARATION
REJECT NUCLEAR DETERRENCE:
AN URGENT CALL TO ACTION

Nuclear deterrence is a doctrine that is used as a justification by nuclear weapon states and their allies for the continued possession and threatened use of nuclear weapons.

Nuclear deterrence is the threat of a nuclear strike in response to a hostile action. However, the nature of the hostile action is often not clearly defined, making possible the use of nuclear weapons in a wide range of circumstances.

Nuclear deterrence threatens the murder of many millions of innocent people, along with severe economic, climate, environmental, agricultural and health consequences beyond the area of attack.

Nuclear deterrence requires massive commitments of resources to the industrial infrastructures and organizations that make up the world's nuclear weapons establishments, its only beneficiaries.

Despite its catastrophic potential, nuclear deterrence is widely, though wrongly, perceived to provide protection to nuclear weapon states, their allies and their citizens.

Nuclear deterrence has numerous major problems:

1. Its power to protect is a dangerous fabrication. The threat or use of nuclear weapons provides no protection against an attack.

2. It assumes rational leaders, but there can be irrational or paranoid leaders on any side of a conflict.

3. Threatening or committing mass murder with nuclear weapons is illegal and criminal. It violates fundamental legal precepts of domestic and international law, threatening the indiscriminate slaughter of innocent people.

4. It is deeply immoral for the same reasons it is illegal: it threatens indiscriminate and grossly disproportionate death and destruction.

5. It diverts human and economic resources desperately needed to meet basic human needs around the world. Globally, approximately $100 billion is spent annually on nuclear forces.

6. It has no effect against non-state extremists, who govern no territory or population.

7. It is vulnerable to cyber attack, sabotage, and human or technical error, which could result in a nuclear strike.

8. It sets an example for additional countries to pursue nuclear weapons for their own nuclear deterrent force.

Its benefits are illusory. Any use of nuclear weapons would be catastrophic.

Nuclear deterrence is discriminatory, anti-democratic and unsustainable. This doctrine must be discredited and replaced with an urgent commitment to achieve global nuclear disarmament. We must change the discourse by speaking truth to power and speaking truth to each other.

Before another nuclear weapon is used, nuclear deterrence must be replaced by humane, legal and moral security strategies. We call upon people everywhere to join us in demanding that the nuclear weapon states and their allies reject nuclear deterrence and negotiate without delay a Nuclear Weapons Convention for the phased, verifiable, irreversible and transparent elimination of all nuclear weapons.[74]

Fifteen Moral Reasons to Abolish Nuclear Weapons

1. Thou shalt not kill.

2. Thou shalt not threaten to slaughter the innocent.

3. Thou shalt not cause unnecessary suffering.

4. Thou shalt not poison the future.

5. Thou shalt not hold hostage cities and their inhabitants.

6. Thou shalt not threaten to destroy civilization.

7. Thou shalt not abandon stewardship of fish and fowl, birds and beasts.

8. Thou shalt not put all of Creation at risk of annihilation.

9. Thou shalt not use weapons that cannot be contained in space or time.

10. Thou shalt not waste resources on weapons—resources that could be far better used for meeting basic human needs.

11. Thou shalt not fail to fulfil one's obligations to negotiate in good faith for nuclear disarmament.

12. Thou shalt not covet thy neighbor's missiles.

13. Thou shalt not worship false idols.

14. Thou shalt not keep silent in the face of the nuclear threat to all we love and treasure.

15. Thou shalt live by the Golden Rule, doing unto others as you would have them do unto you.

Silence Is Indefensible

Arundhati Roy, the great Indian author and activist, said, "There's nothing new or original left to be said about nuclear weapons."[75] Nonetheless, she speaks out because, in her words, "silence would be indefensible."[76] But silence is the norm. We live our day-to-day lives with these weapons capable of destroying our cities, our countries, our civilizations, even our species. How can silence be the norm?

This is what Roy says about nuclear weapons: "Whether they're used or not, they violate everything that is humane. They alter the meaning of life itself. Why do we tolerate them? Why do we tolerate the men who use nuclear weapons to blackmail the entire human race?"[77]

Do we really trust our political leaders and those leaders who might come to power in the future to never unleash the fury of nuclear war? Do we believe that all leaders under all conditions, no matter how rushed or stressed, will refrain from using this power of annihilation? Perhaps we do, and this would explain the widespread complacency and silence.

Perhaps we just feel impotent to change the situation. This resignation is often summed up with the phrase, "the genie cannot be put back into the bottle." So, we have loosed the genie of atomic might on the world, and we appear content to let it roam. We seem to lack the cleverness or motivation even to try to put the genie back into the bottle.

What were the odds of the collapse of the former Soviet Union, or the odds that the Berlin Wall would be peacefully dismantled? Why does virtually no one anticipate big changes such as these on the horizon? While they are rarely foreseen, in hindsight they seem perfectly understandable.

What about the odds of two nuclear armed submarines colliding in the ocean? The chances of this occurring are infinitesimally small. Yet, it happened.[78] Such rare occurrences happen. What are the odds of a nuclear war being unleashed on our planet? Could such a war begin by accident? Could it occur by miscalculation or overreaching? Perhaps the odds are small, but they are not zero and therefore they are above an acceptable level.

Are we silent because we believe that nuclear weapons actually keep us safer? This wouldn't be surprising because we have been taught to believe that we are protected by nuclear weapons. But this isn't the case. Nuclear weapons cannot protect their possessors. They can only be used to inflict massive retaliation and such retaliation is not protection. If nuclear weapons protected their possessors, missile defenses would not be perceived to be needed. But nuclear weapons do not provide protection, and missile defenses are faulty tools for protection, as well. In fact, those that possess nuclear weapons are guaranteed to be targets of someone else's nuclear weapons.

The only safe number of nuclear weapons is zero, and to reach this level will require international cooperation, as with every significant global problem. It will also require leadership and, as the possessors of over 90 percent of the nuclear weapons on the planet, the countries that must lead are the US and Russia. If they fail to lead, the nuclear genie will continue to roam.

Why do we waste our resources on such weapons? Why do we use our scientists in such dehumanizing ways? Why do we debase ourselves with our implicit threats of mass murder?

Are we silent because we are numb? Have we become so distracted that we will not raise our voices because we cannot imagine consequences so horrific? Have we become so fearful of giving voice to our legitimate concerns that we are dumb as well as numb?

Nuclear weapons diminish our humanity, and our silence will condemn us in the eyes of those who will follow us on this planet.

Like Arundhati Roy, I continue to speak out in the belief that silence is indefensible.

Hubris versus Wisdom

Humankind must not be complacent in the face of the threat posed by nuclear weapons. The future of humanity and all life depends upon the outcome of the ongoing struggle between hubris and wisdom.

Hubris is an ancient Greek word meaning extreme arrogance. Wisdom is cautionary good sense.

Hubris is at the heart of Greek tragedy—the arrogant belief that one's power is unassailable. Wisdom counsels that no human fortress is impregnable.

Hubris says some countries can hold onto nuclear weapons and rely upon them for deterrence. Wisdom, in the voice of the survivors of Hiroshima and Nagasaki, says these weapons must be eliminated before they eliminate us.

Hubris says these weapons of annihilation are subject to human control. Wisdom says that humans are fallible creatures, subject to error.

Hubris repeats that we can control our most dangerous technologies. Wisdom says look at what has happened in numerous accidents with nuclear weapons as well as accidents at Three Mile Island, Chernobyl and Fukushima.

Hubris says the spread of nuclear weapons can be contained. Wisdom says that the only sure way to prevent the spread or use of nuclear weapons is to abolish those that now exist.

Hubris says that political leaders will always be rational and avoid the use of nuclear weapons. Wisdom observes that all humans, including political leaders, behave irrationally at times under some circumstances.

Hubris says we can play nuclear roulette with the human future. Wisdom says we have a responsibility to assure there is a human future.

Hubris says that we can control nuclear fire. Wisdom says nuclear weapons will spark wildfires of human suffering and must be eradicated forever from the planet.

The Nuclear Age demands that we conquer complacency with compassion and hubris with wisdom.

Nuclear Zero: Getting to the Finish Line

More than three decades ago, in 1982, the Nuclear Age Peace Foundation was founded. Its vision is a just and peaceful world, free of nuclear weapons. The Foundation's mission is to educate and advocate for peace and a world free of nuclear weapons and to empower peace leaders. So we educate, advocate and empower. We speak out. We are a voice of conscience. We advocate for sane policies and for leadership to achieve a world without nuclear dangers. Our goal is to educate and engage millions of people to move the world to nuclear zero and to peace.

We challenge bad policies, such as the policy of nuclear deterrence, which justifies reliance on nuclear weapons, but has many faults. For nuclear deterrence to work successfully, leaders of nuclear-armed states must be rational at all times and under all circumstances, particularly under conditions of stress when they are least likely to be rational. Also, nuclear deterrence cannot deter those who have no territory to retaliate against or who are suicidal. Thus, nuclear deterrence has no possibility of success against terrorist organizations. To see one of many ways that deterrence can fail, I encourage you to watch the 1964 movie,

Fail-Safe, directed by Sidney Lumet, based upon the 1962 novel of the same name by Eugene Burdick and Harvey Wheeler.[79]

The Foundation also challenges policies that tolerate a two-tier structure of nuclear "haves" and "have-nots." We believe that the ultimate consequences of this two-tier structure will be nuclear proliferation, nuclear terrorism and nuclear war. We also advocate for nuclear policies that reduce risks and move us toward a world without nuclear weapons, policies such as security assurances to non-nuclear weapon states; no first use of nuclear weapons; no launch on warning of nuclear attack; lowering the alert status of nuclear weapons; a comprehensive test ban treaty; and a fissile material cut-off treaty. These are all elements of the critical goal of nuclear weapons abolition and must be viewed in that context.

Scientists tell us that even a small nuclear war with an exchange of 100 Hiroshima-size nuclear weapons could result in reducing warming sunlight and lowering the earth's surface temperature to the lowest in 1,000 years, shortening growing seasons, leading to massive crop failures and widespread global famine.[80] This would be the kind of nuclear war that could occur in South Asia between India and Pakistan. A large-scale nuclear war, the kind that could occur between the US and Russia, would destroy civilization and possibly end the human species and most other complex forms of life on the planet. We all share a responsibility to assure there are no small- or large-scale nuclear wars, but as long as nuclear weapons exist, the possibility of nuclear war also exists.

In October 1962, the world held its collective breath as the Cuban Missile Crisis unfolded. The world was poised on the brink of a nuclear exchange between the US and USSR. John F. Kennedy and Nikita Khrushchev managed to navigate those dangerous currents, but many of their advisors were pushing them toward nuclear war. Decisions on all sides were made with only partial knowledge, which could have resulted in disaster. Robert Kennedy's eye-witness account of the crisis, *Thirteen Days*, is sobering reading.[81]

In 1982, the year the Nuclear Age Peace Foundation was created, there was considerable concern in the world about nuclear dangers. There were more than 60,000 nuclear weapons, nearly all in the arsenals of the US and USSR. More than a million people gathered in Central Park in New York City calling for a nuclear freeze. Of course, they were right to do so. The nuclear arms race was out of control, and the leaders of the US and USSR were not talking to each other. An uncontrollable nuclear arms race coupled with a failure to communicate were and are a recipe for disaster.

By 1986, the nuclear arms race had reached its quantitative peak with over 70,000 nuclear weapons in the world, nearly all in the arsenals of the US and USSR. But by this time Mikhail Gorbachev had come to power in the USSR and was talking about abolishing nuclear weapons by the year 2000. He and President Reagan held a summit meeting in Reykjavik, Iceland in 1986. They seriously discussed their shared goal of ridding the world of nuclear weapons, but their attempt to find their way to zero nuclear weapons foundered on the issue of the Strategic Defense Initiative, now commonly referred to as missile defense. Reagan wanted it; Gorbachev didn't.

Since 1986, we have made progress in substantially reducing nuclear arsenals to the current number of some 16,000 worldwide, having shed more than 54,000 nuclear weapons. Of the 7,200 nuclear weapons in the US arsenal, about 2,500 are awaiting dismantlement and approximately 2,000 are deployed, a somewhat higher number than the 1,780 deployed nuclear weapons in Russia. The US and Russia have agreed that they will each reduce their deployed strategic weapons to 1,550 by the year 2018. Neither country has conducted an atmospheric or underground nuclear weapon test since 1992 (other than underground subcritical nuclear tests in which the nuclear material does not reach the criticality necessary for a nuclear chain reaction).

Since the breakup of the Soviet Union in 1991, the US and Russia have been, until recently, on relatively positive terms. Through solid US negotiating in the early 1990s, the Ukraine, Kazakhstan and Belarus agreed to give up the nuclear arsenals that the former Soviet Union had left on their territories and to give these weapons over to Russia for dismantlement.

It was a significant event in 1996 when US Secretary of Defense William Perry met with the Russian and Ukrainian Defense Ministers at a former missile base in Ukraine to plant sunflowers. The nuclear abolition movement adopted the sunflower as a symbol of a nuclear weapon-free world. The sunflower symbolizes everything that a nuclear-armed missile is not, being natural, nutritious, healthy, beautiful, grounded in the earth and powered by the sun.[82]

We have come a long way, but we haven't reached the finish line, which is a world with zero nuclear weapons. The challenge we face now is to educate decision makers and the public that the dangers of nuclear weapons have not gone away. There are still many flash points of nuclear danger in the world: India-Pakistan, North Korea, and Ukraine. Other issues include the continued possession of nuclear weapons by the UK and France, the possession of nuclear weapons by Israel with the incentive for nuclear proliferation this creates in the Middle East, and the relationship of the nuclear energy fuel cycle to nuclear proliferation.

The greatest problem related to nuclear weapons is not that Iran or another country might develop such weapons, although proliferation concerns are certainly important. The greatest problem remains that the countries with nuclear weapons are not taking seriously their obligations to end the nuclear weapons threat to humanity and achieve nuclear zero. Nuclear weapons do not make their possessors more secure. When a country has nuclear weapons or seeks to acquire them, that country will also be a target of nuclear weapons. This goes for the US, Russia, and all other countries with nuclear weapons, as well as those seeking to develop them. Nuclear weapons possession turns cities and countries into targets for mass annihilation.

What shall we do to advance to zero? In the spirit of Reagan and Gorbachev, the US and Russia must lead the way. They still possess over 90 percent of the nuclear weapons in the world. President Obama requested a study of possible reduction of deployed strategic nuclear weapons at three levels: 1,000-1,100 weapons; 700-800 weapons; and 300-400 weapons.[83] This is significant. It is worth advocating for US leadership to reduce the US nuclear arsenal to the lower level, to 300 nuclear weapons, as a next step. But this would not be the desired end result. First, it is not low enough; it is not zero. It still would be more than enough to destroy civilization. Second, it is unilateral; it must be bilateral and moving toward multilateral.

Going down to 300 deployed strategic nuclear weapons would be a significant reduction, but it should be a joint endeavor with Russia. To get Russia to join us in this next step will require the US to move its missile defense installations away from the Russian borders, so that Russia does not feel threatened by these defenses, particularly at lower levels of offensive weapons. US officials tell Russia not to worry about these missile defense installations, but the Russians are wary. It is easy to understand this if one imagines the Russians placing missile defense installations on the Canadian border and telling the US not to worry. Missile defenses, if they are deemed necessary, must be a joint project, just as reduction in the numbers of offensive nuclear weapons must be a joint project.

The US and Russia must cooperate on continuing to reduce their nuclear arsenals for their own security and for global security. At the level of 300 deployed strategic nuclear weapons each, they would then be in a position of rough parity with the other nuclear weapon states and in a position to effectively negotiate a Nuclear Weapons Convention for the phased, verifiable, irreversible and transparent elimination of nuclear weapons. The number that matters most in the nuclear disarmament arena is zero. It is the most secure and stable number of nuclear weapons. It must be achieved carefully and in phases, but it must be achieved for the benefit of our children, grandchildren and all future generations.

The Nuclear Zero Lawsuits:
Taking Nuclear Weapons to Court

Nuclear weapons remain the most urgent threat confronting humanity. So long as they exist, there is the very real chance they will be used by accident, miscalculation or design. These weapons threaten everyone and everything we love and treasure. They are fearsome destructive devices that kill indiscriminately and cause unnecessary suffering. No man, woman or child is safe from the fury of these weapons, now or in the future. Nor is any country safe from them, no matter how powerful or how much it threatens nuclear retaliation.

Given the extreme dangers of nuclear weapons, we might ask: why isn't more being done to eliminate them? There has been talk and promises, but little action by the nine nuclear-armed nations—United States, Russia, United Kingdom, France, China, Israel, India, Pakistan and North Korea. All nine countries are modernizing their nuclear arsenals.

One small Pacific nation, the Republic of the Marshall Islands, has decided to take legal action against the nine nuclear-armed countries, which are threatening our common future. As Tony de Brum, Foreign Minister of the

Marshall Islands, points out, "The continued existence of nuclear weapons and the terrible risk they pose to the world threatens us all."

To understand the nature of the legal actions taken by the Marshall Islands, it is necessary to go back in time. In 1968, the nuclear Non-Proliferation Treaty (NPT) was opened for signatures; two years later, in 1970, it entered into force. The treaty seeks to stop the further spread of nuclear weapons, but it does more. It also obligates its parties to level the playing field by negotiating in good faith for an end to the nuclear arms race and for nuclear disarmament. This treaty currently has 191 parties signed on, including five nuclear weapon states and 186 non-nuclear weapon parties.

The Marshall Islands is taking its case to the International Court of Justice in The Hague and, in addition, filing separately against the US in US Federal District Court in Northern California. The lawsuits argue that the nuclear disarmament obligations apply to all nine nuclear-armed states, either due to the obligations of the nuclear-armed states that are parties to the NPT or as a matter of customary international law. The courts are being asked in these Nuclear Zero Lawsuits to provide declaratory and injunctive relief, by declaring that the nuclear weapon states are in breach of their nuclear disarmament obligations under international law and ordering them to begin negotiating in good faith to achieve a cessation of the nuclear arms race and a world with zero nuclear weapons.

The Marshall Islands has shown courage and boldness by taking action in filing these lawsuits. It is a country that knows firsthand the consequences of nuclear detonations. Between 1946 and 1958, the US conducted 67 nuclear weapon tests in the Marshall Islands. These tests had an equivalent explosive force of 1.6 Hiroshima bombs being detonated daily for 12 years. The Marshall Islanders paid a heavy price in terms of their health, well-being and the radioactive contamination of their lands for these destructive tests.

Now this small island nation of 70,000 inhabitants is standing up against nine of the most powerful countries on the planet. It is "David" against the nine nuclear "Goliaths." Instead of a slingshot, it is using the law; and its field of nonviolent battle is the courtroom.

The Marshall Islands is, in effect, challenging the nuclear weapon countries to be honorable and fulfill their obligations not only to the rest of the countries that signed the nuclear Non-Proliferation Treaty, but to all humanity.

The Republic of the Marshall Islands is offering us a way to live on a planet that is not threatened by nuclear catastrophe due to human fallibility or malevolence. This courageous small island country deserves our strong and unwavering support.

To follow the Marshall Islands Nuclear Zero lawsuits, visit www.nuclearzero.org.

Ten Reasons to Abolish Nuclear Weapons

There are many reasons to favor the abolition of nuclear weapons. Each of the ten reasons listed below is a powerful argument against the possession, threat or use of nuclear weapons. Taken together, they make an irrefutable case for abolishing nuclear weapons.

1. They are long-distance killing machines incapable of discriminating between soldiers and civilians, the aged and the newly born, or between men, women and children. As such, they are instruments of dehumanization as well as annihilation.

2. They threaten the destruction of cities, countries and civilization, of all that we have created, of all that is human, of all that exists. Nuclear war could cause deadly climate change and nuclear famine, putting human existence at risk.

3. They threaten to foreclose the future, negating our common responsibility to future generations.

4. They make cowards of their possessors, and in their use there can be no decency or honor. This was recognized by most of the leading generals and admirals of World War II, including Dwight Eisenhower, Hap Arnold and William Leahy.

5. They divide the world's nations into nuclear "haves" and "have-nots," bestowing false and unwarranted prestige and privilege on those that possess them.

6. They are a distortion of science and technology, siphoning off our scientific and technological resources and twisting our knowledge of nature to destructive purposes.

7. They mock international law, displacing it with an allegiance to raw power. The International Court of Justice has found that the threat or use of nuclear weapons is generally illegal and any use that violates international humanitarian law (the laws of war) would be illegal. It is virtually impossible to imagine a threat or use of nuclear weapons that would not violate international humanitarian law by failing to discriminate between soldiers and civilians, causing unnecessary suffering, or being disproportionate to a preceding attack.

8. They waste our resources on the development of instruments of annihilation. The United States alone has spent over $7.5 trillion on nuclear weapons and their delivery systems since the onset of the Nuclear Age.

9. They concentrate power in the hands of a small group of individuals and, in doing so, undermine democracy. In each country that possesses nuclear weapons, the decision to use them is left to a few powerful individuals. By turning over civilization-destroying power to a few individuals, democracy is usurped by the leaders of the national security state.

10. They are morally abhorrent, as recognized by virtually every religious organization, and their mere existence corrupts our humanity.

Awakening America Before
It Is Too Late

*The shaft of the arrow had been feathered with one of the
eagle's own plumes. We often give our enemies the means of
our own destruction."*

~Aesop's Fables

America has been warned in every conceivable fashion
that its nuclear weapons will bring it to a bad end.

It was warned by scientists on its own atomic bomb project, even before it bombed Hiroshima and Nagasaki, and it
was warned by the destruction of those cities.

It was warned by Mahatma Gandhi that it was too early
to see what nuclear weapons would do the soul of the attacking nation.

It was warned by Albert Einstein that we must change
our modes of thinking or face "unparalleled catastrophe."

It has been warned by Nobel Laureates, by generals and
admirals, by small countries and large ones.

It was warned by Bertrand Russell, J. Robert Oppenheimer and Linus Pauling.

It was warned by the Cuban missile crisis, and by other near disasters.

It was warned by the survivors of Hiroshima and Nagasaki that human beings and nuclear weapons cannot co-exist.

It has been warned by religious leaders, including Archbishop Desmond Tutu, the XIVth Dalai Lama, and Pope Francis, that nuclear weapons jeopardize all creation.

It has been warned by political leaders, including Ronald Reagan and Mikhail Gorbachev, that nuclear war cannot be won and must never be fought.

It was warned by a former head of the US Strategic Command, General George Lee Butler, that "we cannot at once keep sacred the miracle of existence and hold sacrosanct the capacity to destroy it."[84]

It was warned by the mayors of cities and by earnest citizen groups.

It was warned by "duck and cover" drills, fall-out shelters and false alerts.

It has been warned and warned until the sirens should be screaming in the White House and in the halls of Congress.

But we live in a time of political leaders lacking a moral compass, of political leaders unable to change their thinking or to shed their hubris.

Since nuclear weapons are the most cowardly weapon ever created, we live in a time of leaders marked by a significant courage-deficit.

All signs suggest that we are headed toward disaster, toward a world in which America itself could be sacrificed at the altar of its hubris.

We have become too attached to our double standards, to a world of nuclear "haves" and "have-nots."

We spend on nuclear weapons and their delivery systems what it would cost to feed the world's hungry, shelter the world's homeless, care for the world's sick and infirm, and educate the world's children.

In our comfortable reliance on our military might, we have failed to grasp that nuclear weapons are a far more powerful tool in the hands of the weak than in the hands of the strong.

We have failed to grasp that America cannot afford to again use nuclear weapons, while extremist groups are eager to obtain these weapons and use them against us.

We have failed to grasp that there is no defense against nuclear weapons, as we throw money into missile defenses like a helpless giant.

America stands at increasing risk that its great cities will be destroyed by nuclear weapons.

Our cities, our economy and our pride will fall together.

Should this happen, America will bellow and flail, flames will shoot from its nostrils, and the survivors will wonder how America was brought so low.

Looking back, some will remember with dismay the many, many warnings. Others will say that it was karma.

This is a glimpse into a possible future. It is yet another warning. The worst has not yet happened.

It is not too late for America to wake up, to fulfill its obligations for the total elimination of nuclear weapons, and to lead the countries of the world to a nuclear weapon-free planet.

It is late, but it is not too late. America may still wake up, and if it does it will be because people have not given up on America or on a human future.

It will be because ordinary Americans do not have the courage-deficit that many of our leaders have so readily and consistently displayed.

It will be because the voices of the people rise up and demand change and because we become the leaders we have been waiting for.

It will be because we have succeeded in leading the world to negotiate a new treaty for the elimination of nuclear weapons.

It will be because we have created the conditions to achieve nuclear zero.

THE MERRY-GO-ROUND

The end could begin with a missile launched by accident.
And then the response would be deliberate, as would be
the counter-response, and on and on until we were all

gone.

Or, it could be deliberate from the outset, an act
of madness by a suicidal leader, setting the end in motion.

First, the blasts and mushroom clouds. Then the fires
and burning cities and the winds driving the fires, turning
humans into projectiles, and all of it mixed with deadly
radiation. Finally, for the last act, the soot from destroyed
cities rising into the upper stratosphere, blocking the sunlight
and the temperatures falling into a frozen Ice Age, followed
by mass starvation.

If any humans were left to name it, they might call it
"Global Hiroshima," but none would be left.
It would be ugly for a while, eerily still and silent
for some stretch of time, but no one would be there
to observe. Still, the Earth would go on rotating
around the sun and the universe would go on expanding.

Only we humans would be off the not-so-merry-go-round.

APPENDICES

Appendix A

REMARKS OF PRESIDENT BARACK OBAMA
Hradĉany Square
Prague, Czech Republic
April 5, 2009

Thank you for this wonderful welcome. Thank you to the people of Prague. And thank you to the people of the Czech Republic. Today, I am proud to stand here with you in the middle of this great city, in the center of Europe. And - to paraphrase one my predecessors - I am also proud to be the man who brought Michelle Obama to Prague.

I have learned over many years to appreciate the good company and good humor of the Czech people in my hometown of Chicago. Behind me is a statue of a hero of the Czech people - Tomas Masaryk. In 1918, after America had pledged its support for Czech independence, Masaryk spoke to a crowd in Chicago that was estimated to be over 100,000. I don't think I can match Masaryk's record, but I'm honored to follow his footsteps from Chicago to Prague.

For over a thousand years, Prague has set itself apart from any other city in any other place. You have known war and peace. You have seen empires rise and fall. You have led revolutions in the arts and science, in politics and poetry. Through it all, the people of Prague have insisted on pursuing their own path, and defining their own destiny. And this city - this Golden City which is both ancient and youthful - stands as a living monument to your unconquerable spirit.

When I was born, the world was divided, and our nations were faced with very different circumstances. Few people would have predicted that someone like me would one day become an American President. Few people would have predicted that an American President would one day be permitted to speak to an audience like this in Prague. And few would have imagined that the Czech Republic would become a free nation, a member of NATO, and a leader of a united Europe. Those ideas would have been dismissed as dreams.

We are here today because enough people ignored the voices who told them that the world could not change.

We are here today because of the courage of those who stood up - and took risks - to say that freedom is a right for all people, no matter what side of a wall they live on, and no matter what they look like.

We are here today because of the Prague Spring - because the simple and principled pursuit of liberty and opportunity shamed those who relied on the power of tanks and arms to put down the will of the people.

We are here today because twenty years ago, the people of this city took to the streets to claim the promise of a new day, and the fundamental human rights that had been denied to them for far too long. Sametová revoluce - the Velvet Revolution taught us many things. It showed us that peaceful protest could shake the foundation of an empire, and expose the emptiness of an ideology. It showed us that small countries can play a pivotal role in world events, and that young people can lead the way in overcoming old conflicts. And it proved that moral leadership is more powerful than any weapon.

That is why I am speaking to you in the center of a Europe that is peaceful, united and free - because ordinary people believed that divisions could be bridged; that walls could come down; and that peace could prevail.

We are here today because Americans and Czechs believed against all odds that today could be possible.

We share this common history. But now this generation - our generation - cannot stand still. We, too, have a choice to make. As the world has become less divided it has become more inter-connected. And we have seen events move faster than our ability to control them - a global economy in crisis; a changing climate; the persistent dangers of old conflicts, new threats and the spread of catastrophic weapons.

None of these challenges can be solved quickly or easily. But all of them demand that we listen to one another and work together; that we focus on our common interests, not our occasional differences; and that we reaffirm our shared values, which are stronger than any force that could drive us apart. That is the work that we must carry on. That is the work that I have come to Europe to begin.

To renew our prosperity, we need action coordinated across borders. That means investments to create new jobs. That means resisting the walls of protectionism that stand in the way of growth. That means a change in our financial system, with new rules to prevent abuse and future crisis. And we have an obligation to our common prosperity and our common humanity to extend a hand to those emerging markets and impoverished people who are suffering the most, which is why we set aside over a trillion dollars for the International Monetary Fund earlier this week.

To protect our planet, now is the time to change the way that we use energy. Together, we must confront climate change by ending the world's dependence on fossil fuels, tapping the power of new sources of energy like the wind and sun, and calling upon all nations to do their part. And I pledge to you that in this global effort, the United States is now ready to lead.

To provide for our common security, we must strengthen our alliance. NATO was founded sixty years ago, after Communism took over Czechoslovakia. That was when the free world learned too late that it could not afford division. So we came together to forge the strongest alliance that the world has ever known. And we stood shoulder to shoulder - year after year, decade after decade - until an Iron Curtain was lifted, and freedom spread like flowing water.

This marks the tenth year of NATO membership for the Czech Republic. I know that many times in the 20th century, decisions were made without you at the table. Great powers let you down, or determined your destiny without your voice being heard. I am here to say that the United States will never turn its back on the people of this nation. We are bound by shared values, shared history, and the enduring promise of our alliance. NATO's Article 5 states it clearly: an attack on one is an attack on all. That is a promise for our time, and for all time.

The people of the Czech Republic kept that promise after America was attacked, thousands were killed on our soil, and NATO responded. NATO's mission in Afghanistan is fundamental to the safety of people on both sides of the Atlantic. We are targeting the same al Qaeda terrorists who have struck from New York to London, and helping the Afghan people take responsibility for their future. We are demonstrating that free nations can make common cause on behalf of our common security. And I want you to know that we Americans honor the sacrifices of the Czech people in this endeavor, and mourn the loss of those you have lost.

No alliance can afford to stand still. We must work together as NATO members so that we have contingency plans in place to deal with new threats, wherever they may come from. We must strengthen our cooperation with one another, and with other nations and institutions around the world, to confront dangers that recognize no borders. And we must pursue constructive relations with Russia on issues of common concern.

One of those issues that I will focus on today is fundamental to our nations, and to the peace and security of the world - the future of nuclear weapons in the 21st century.

The existence of thousands of nuclear weapons is the most dangerous legacy of the Cold War. No nuclear war was fought between the United States and the Soviet Union, but generations lived with the knowledge that their world could be erased in a single flash of light. Cities like Prague that had existed for centuries would have ceased to exist.

Today, the Cold War has disappeared but thousands of those weapons have not. In a strange turn of history, the threat of global nuclear war has gone down, but the risk of a nuclear attack has gone up. More nations have acquired these weapons. Testing has continued. Black markets trade in nuclear secrets and materials. The technology to build a bomb has spread. Terrorists are determined to buy, build or steal one. Our efforts to contain these dangers are centered in a global non-proliferation regime, but as more people and nations break the rules, we could reach the point when the center cannot hold.

This matters to all people, everywhere. One nuclear weapon exploded in one city - be it New York or Moscow, Islamabad or Mumbai, Tokyo or Tel Aviv, Paris or Prague -

could kill hundreds of thousands of people. And no matter where it happens, there is no end to what the consequences may be - for our global safety, security, society, economy, and ultimately our survival.

Some argue that the spread of these weapons cannot be checked - that we are destined to live in a world where more nations and more people possess the ultimate tools of destruction. This fatalism is a deadly adversary. For if we believe that the spread of nuclear weapons is inevitable, then we are admitting to ourselves that the use of nuclear weapons is inevitable.

Just as we stood for freedom in the 20th century, we must stand together for the right of people everywhere to live free from fear in the 21st. And as a nuclear power - as the only nuclear power to have used a nuclear weapon - the United States has a moral responsibility to act. We cannot succeed in this endeavor alone, but we can lead it.

So today, I state clearly and with conviction America's commitment to seek the peace and security of a world without nuclear weapons. This goal will not be reached quickly - perhaps not in my lifetime. It will take patience and persistence. But now we, too, must ignore the voices who tell us that the world cannot change.

First, the United States will take concrete steps toward a world without nuclear weapons.

To put an end to Cold War thinking, we will reduce the role of nuclear weapons in our national security strategy and urge others to do the same. Make no mistake: as long as these weapons exist, we will maintain a safe, secure and effective arsenal to deter any adversary, and guarantee that defense to our allies - including the Czech Republic. But we will begin the work of reducing our arsenal.

To reduce our warheads and stockpiles, we will negotiate a new strategic arms reduction treaty with Russia this year. President Medvedev and I began this process in London, and will seek a new agreement by the end of this year that is legally binding, and sufficiently bold. This will set the stage for further cuts, and we will seek to include all nuclear weapons states in this endeavor.

To achieve a global ban on nuclear testing, my Administration will immediately and aggressively pursue U.S. ratification of the Comprehensive Test Ban Treaty. After more than five decades of talks, it is time for the testing of nuclear weapons to finally be banned.

And to cut off the building blocks needed for a bomb, the United States will seek a new treaty that verifiably ends the production of fissile materials intended for use in state nuclear weapons. If we are serious about stopping the spread of these weapons, then we should put an end to the dedicated production of weapons grade materials that create them.

Second, together, we will strengthen the nuclear Non-Proliferation Treaty as a basis for cooperation.

The basic bargain is sound: countries with nuclear weapons will move toward disarmament, countries without nuclear weapons will not acquire them; and all countries can access peaceful nuclear energy. To strengthen the Treaty, we should embrace several principles. We need more resources and authority to strengthen international inspections. We need real and immediate consequences for countries caught breaking the rules or trying to leave the Treaty without cause.

And we should build a new framework for civil nuclear cooperation, including an international fuel bank, so that countries can access peaceful power without increasing the risks of proliferation. That must be the right of every nation that renounces nuclear weapons, especially developing countries embarking on peaceful programs. No approach will succeed if it is based on the denial of rights to nations that play by the rules. We must harness the power of nuclear energy on behalf of our efforts to combat climate change, and to advance opportunity for all people.

We go forward with no illusions. Some will break the rules, but that is why we need a structure in place that ensures that when any nation does, they will face consequences. This morning, we were reminded again why we need a new and more rigorous approach to address this threat. North Korea broke the rules once more by testing a rocket that could be used for a long range missile.

This provocation underscores the need for action - not just this afternoon at the UN Security Council, but in our determination to prevent the spread of these weapons. Rules must be binding. Violations must be punished. Words must mean something. The world must stand together to prevent the spread of these weapons. Now is the time for a strong international response. North Korea must know that the path to security and respect will never come through threats and illegal weapons. And all nations must come together to build a stronger, global regime.

Iran has yet to build a nuclear weapon. And my Administration will seek engagement with Iran based upon mutual interests and mutual respect, and we will present a clear choice. We want Iran to take its rightful place in the community of nations, politically and economically. We will support Iran's right to peaceful nuclear energy with rigorous inspections. That is a path that the Islamic Republic can take. Or the government can choose increased isolation, international pressure, and a potential nuclear arms race in the region that will increase insecurity for all.

Let me be clear: Iran's nuclear and ballistic missile activity poses a real threat, not just to the United States, but to Iran's neighbors and our allies. The Czech Republic and

Poland have been courageous in agreeing to host a defense against these missiles. As long as the threat from Iran persists, we intend to go forward with a missile defense system that is cost-effective and proven. If the Iranian threat is eliminated, we will have a stronger basis for security, and the driving force for missile defense construction in Europe at this time will be removed.

Finally, we must ensure that terrorists never acquire a nuclear weapon.

This is the most immediate and extreme threat to global security. One terrorist with a nuclear weapon could unleash massive destruction. Al Qaeda has said that it seeks a bomb. And we know that there is unsecured nuclear material across the globe. To protect our people, we must act with a sense of purpose without delay.

Today, I am announcing a new international effort to secure all vulnerable nuclear material around the world within four years. We will set new standards, expand our cooperation with Russia, and pursue new partnerships to lock down these sensitive materials.

We must also build on our efforts to break up black markets, detect and intercept materials in transit, and use financial tools to disrupt this dangerous trade. Because this threat will be lasting, we should come together to turn efforts such as the Proliferation Security Initiative and the Global Initiative to Combat Nuclear Terrorism into durable international institutions. And we should start by having a Global Summit on Nuclear Security that the United States will host within the next year.

I know that there are some who will question whether we can act on such a broad agenda. There are those who doubt whether true international cooperation is possible, given the inevitable differences among nations. And there are those who hear talk of a world without nuclear weapons and doubt whether it is worth setting a goal that seems impossible to achieve.

But make no mistake: we know where that road leads. When nations and peoples allow themselves to be defined by their differences, the gulf between them widens. When we fail to pursue peace, then it stays forever beyond our grasp. To denounce or shrug off a call for cooperation is an easy and cowardly thing. That is how wars begin. That is where human progress ends.

There is violence and injustice in our world that must be confronted. We must confront it not by splitting apart, but by standing together as free nations, as free people. I know that a call to arms can stir the souls of men and women more than a call to lay them down. But that is why the voices for peace and progress must be raised together.

Those are the voices that still echo through the streets of Prague. Those are the ghosts of 1968. Those were the joyful sounds of the Velvet Revolution. Those were the Czechs who helped bring down a nuclear-armed empire without firing a shot.

Human destiny will be what we make of it. Here, in Prague, let us honor our past by reaching for a better future. Let us bridge our divisions, build upon our hopes, and accept our responsibility to leave this world more prosperous and more peaceful than we found it. Thank you.

Appendix B

In the tragic situation which confronts humanity, we feel that scientists should assemble in conference to appraise the perils that have arisen as a result of the development of weapons of mass destruction, and to discuss a resolution in the spirit of the appended draft.

We are speaking on this occasion, not as members of this or that nation, continent, or creed, but as human beings, members of the species Man, whose continued existence is in doubt. The world is full of conflicts; and, overshadowing all minor conflicts, the titanic struggle between Communism and anti-Communism.

Almost everybody who is politically conscious has strong feelings about one or more of these issues; but we want you, if you can, to set aside such feelings and consider yourselves only as members of a biological species which has had a remarkable history, and whose disappearance none of us can desire.

We shall try to say no single word which should appeal to one group rather than to another. All, equally, are in peril, and, if the peril is understood, there is hope that they may collectively avert it.

We have to learn to think in a new way. We have to learn to ask ourselves, not what steps can be taken to give military victory to whatever group we prefer, for there no longer are such steps; the question we have to ask ourselves is: what steps can be taken to prevent a military contest of which the issue must be disastrous to all parties?

The general public, and even many men in positions of authority, have not realized what would be involved in a war with nuclear bombs. The general public still thinks in terms of the obliteration of cities. It is understood that the new bombs are more powerful than the old, and that, while one A-bomb could obliterate Hiroshima, one H-bomb could obliterate the largest cities, such as London, New York, and Moscow.

No doubt in an H-bomb war great cities would be obliterated. But this is one of the minor disasters that would have to be faced. If everybody in London, New York, and Moscow were exterminated, the world might, in the course of a few centuries, recover from the blow. But we now know, especially since the Bikini test, that nuclear bombs can gradually spread destruction over a very much wider area than had been supposed.

It is stated on very good authority that a bomb can now be manufactured which will be 2,500 times as powerful as that which destroyed Hiroshima. Such a bomb, if exploded near the ground or under water, sends radio-active particles into the upper air. They sink gradually and reach the surface of the earth in the form of a deadly dust or rain. It was this dust which infected the Japanese fishermen and their catch of fish. No one knows how widely such lethal radioactive particles might be diffused, but the best authorities are unanimous in saying that a war with H-bombs might possibly put an end to the human race. It is feared that if many H-bombs are used there will be universal death, sudden only for a minority, but for the majority a slow torture of disease and disintegration.

Many warnings have been uttered by eminent men of science and by authorities in military strategy. None of them will say that the worst results are certain. What they do say is that these results are possible, and no one can be sure that they will not be realized. We have not yet found that the views of experts on this question depend in any degree upon their politics or prejudices. They depend only, so far as our researches have revealed, upon the extent of the particular expert's knowledge. We have found that the men who know most are the most gloomy.

Here, then, is the problem which we present to you, stark and dreadful and inescapable: Shall we put an end to the human race; or shall mankind renounce war? People will not face this alternative because it is so difficult to abolish war.

The abolition of war will demand distasteful limitations of national sovereignty. But what perhaps impedes understanding of the situation more than anything else is that the term "mankind" feels vague and abstract. People scarcely realize in imagination that the danger is to themselves and their children and their grandchildren, and not only to a dimly apprehended humanity. They can scarcely bring themselves to grasp that they, individually, and those whom they love are in imminent danger of perishing agonizingly. And so they hope that perhaps war may be allowed to continue provided modern weapons are prohibited.

This hope is illusory. Whatever agreements not to use H-bombs had been reached in time of peace, they would no longer be considered binding in time of war, and both sides would set to work to manufacture H-bombs as soon as war broke out, for, if one side manufactured the bombs and the other did not, the side that manufactured them would inevitably be victorious.

Although an agreement to renounce nuclear weapons as part of a general reduction of armaments would not afford an ultimate solution, it would serve certain important purposes. First, any agreement between East and West is to the good in so far as it tends to diminish tension. Second, the abolition of thermo-nuclear weapons, if each side believed that the other had carried it out sincerely, would lessen the fear of a sudden attack in the style of Pearl Harbour, which at present keeps both sides in a state of nervous apprehension. We should, therefore, welcome such an agreement though only as a first step.

Most of us are not neutral in feeling, but, as human beings, we have to remember that, if the issues between East and West are to be decided in any manner that can give any possible satisfaction to anybody, whether Communist or anti-Communist, whether Asian or European or American, whether White or Black, then these issues must not be decided by war. We should wish this to be understood, both in the East and in the West.

There lies before us, if we choose, continual progress in happiness, knowledge, and wisdom. Shall we, instead, choose death, because we cannot forget our quarrels? We appeal as human beings to human beings: Remember your humanity, and forget the rest. If you can do so, the way lies open to a new Paradise; if you cannot, there lies before you the risk of universal death.

Resolution:

We invite this Congress, and through it the scientists of the world and the general public, to subscribe to the following resolution:

"In view of the fact that in any future world war nuclear weapons will certainly be employed, and that such weapons threaten the continued existence of mankind, we urge the governments of the world to realize, and to acknowledge publicly, that their purpose cannot be furthered by a world war, and we urge them, consequently, to find peaceful means for the settlement of all matters of dispute between them."

Max Born
Percy W. Bridgman
Albert Einstein
Leopold Infeld
Frederic Joliot-Curie
Herman J. Muller
Linus Pauling
Cecil F. Powell
Joseph Rotblat
Bertrand Russell
Hideki Yukawa

Appendix C

REMEMBER YOUR HUMANITY
Acceptance and Nobel Lecture, 1995
Joseph Rotblat

A t this momentous event in my life - the acceptance of the Nobel Peace Prize - I want to speak as a scientist, but also as a human being. From my earliest days I had a passion for science. But science, the exercise of the supreme power of the human intellect, was always linked in my mind with benefit to people. I saw science as being in harmony with humanity. I did not imagine that the second half of my life would be spent on efforts to avert a mortal danger to humanity created by science.

The practical release of nuclear energy was the outcome of many years of experimental and theoretical research. It had great potential for the common good. But the first the general public learned about the discovery was the news of the destruction of Hiroshima by the atom bomb. A splendid achievement of science and technology had turned malign. Science became identified with death and destruction.

It is painful to me to admit that this depiction of science was deserved. The decision to use the atom bomb on Japanese cities, and the consequent buildup of enormous nuclear arsenals, was made by governments, on the basis of political and military perceptions. But scientists on both sides of the iron curtain played a very significant role in maintaining the momentum of the nuclear arms race throughout the four decades of the Cold War.

The role of scientists in the nuclear arms race was expressed bluntly by Lord Zuckerman, for many years Chief Scientific Adviser to the British Government:[1]

> *When it comes to nuclear weapons ... it is the man in the laboratory who at the start proposes that for this or that arcane reason it would be useful to improve an old or to devise a new nuclear warhead. It is he, the technician, not the commander in the field, who is at the heart of the arms race.*

Long before the terrifying potential of the arms race was recognized, there was a widespread instinctive abhorrence of nuclear weapons, and a strong desire to get rid of them. Indeed, the very first resolution of the General Assembly of the United Nations - adopted unanimously - called for the elimination of nuclear weapons. But the world was then polarized by the bitter ideological struggle between East and West. There was no chance to meet this call. The chief task was to stop the arms race before it brought utter disaster. However, after the collapse of communism and the disintegration of the Soviet Union, any rationale for having nuclear weapons disappeared. The quest for their total elimination could be resumed. But the nuclear powers still cling tenaciously to their weapons.

Let me remind you that nuclear disarmament is not just an ardent desire of the people, as expressed in many resolutions of the United Nations. It is a legal commitment by the five official nuclear states, entered into when they signed the Non-Proliferation Treaty. Only a few months ago, when the indefinite extension of the Treaty was agreed, the nuclear powers committed themselves again to complete nuclear disarmament. This is still their declared goal. But the declarations are not matched by their policies, and this divergence seems to be intrinsic.

Since the end of the Cold War two main nuclear powers have begun to make big reductions in their nuclear arsenals. Each of them is dismantling about 2,000 nuclear warheads a year. If this program continued, all nuclear warheads could be dismantled in little over ten years from now. We have the technical means to create a nuclear-weapon-free world in about a decade. Alas, the present program does not provide for this. When the START 2 treaty has been implemented - and remember it has not yet been ratified - we will be left with some 15,000 nuclear warheads, active and in reserve. Fifteen thousand weapons with an average yield of 20 Hiroshima bombs.

Unless there is a change in the basic philosophy, we will not see a reduction of nuclear arsenals to zero for a very long time, if ever. The present basic philosophy is nuclear deterrence. This was stated clearly in the US Nuclear Posture Review which concluded: *"Post-Cold War environment requires nuclear deterrence,"*[2] and this is echoed by other nuclear states. Nuclear weapons are kept as a hedge against some unspecified dangers.

This policy is simply an inertial continuation from the Cold War era. The Cold War is over but Cold War thinking survives. Then, we were told that a world war was prevented by the existence of nuclear weapons. Now, we are told that nuclear weapons prevent all kinds of war. These are arguments that purport to prove a negative. I am reminded of a story told in my boyhood at the time when radio communication began.

Two wise men were arguing about the ancient civilization in their respective countries. One said: 'my country has a long history of technological development: we have carried out deep excavations and found a wire, which shows that already in the old days we had the telegraph'. The other man retorted: 'we too made excavations; we dug much deeper than you and found ... nothing, which proves that already in those days we had wireless communication'!

There is no direct evidence that nuclear weapons prevented a world war. Conversely, it is known that they nearly caused one. The most terrifying moment in my life was October 1962, during the Cuban Missile Crisis. I did not know all the facts - we have learned only recently how close we were to war - but I knew enough to make me tremble. The lives of millions of people were about to end abruptly; millions of others were to suffer a lingering death; much of our civilization was to be destroyed. It all hung on the decision of one man, Nikita Khrushchev: would he or would he not yield to the U.S. ultimatum?[3] This is the reality of nuclear weapons: they may trigger a world war; a war which, unlike previous ones, destroys all of civilization.

As for the assertion that nuclear weapons prevent wars, how many more wars are needed to refute this argument? Tens of millions have died in the many wars that have taken place since 1945. In a number of them nuclear states were directly involved. In two they were actually defeated. Having nuclear weapons was of no use to them.

To sum up, there is no evidence that a world without nuclear weapons would be a dangerous world. On the contrary, it would be a safer world, as I will show later.

We are told that the possession of nuclear weapons - in some cases even the testing of these weapons - is essential for national security. But this argument can be made by other countries as well. If the militarily most powerful - and least threatened - states need nuclear weapons for their security, how can one deny such security to countries that are truly insecure? The present nuclear policy is a recipe for proliferation. It is a policy for disaster.

To prevent this disaster - for the sake of humanity - we must get rid of all nuclear weapons.

Achieving this goal will take time, but it will never happen unless we make a start. Some essential steps towards it can be taken now. Several studies, and a number of public statements by senior military and political personalities, testify that - except for disputes between the present nuclear states - all military conflicts, as well as threats to peace, can be dealt with using conventional weapons. This means that the only function of nuclear weapons, while they exist, is to deter a nuclear attack. All nuclear weapon states should now recognize that this is so, and declare - in Treaty form - that they will never be the first to use nuclear weapons. This would open the way to the gradual, mutual reduction of nuclear arsenals, down to zero. It would also open the way for a Nuclear Weapons Convention. This would be universal - it would prohibit all possession of nuclear weapons.

We will need to work out the necessary verification system to safeguard the Convention. A Pugwash study produced suggestions on these matters.[4] The mechanisms for negotiating such a Convention already exists. Entering into negotiations does not commit the parties. There is no reason why they should not begin now. If not now, when?

So I ask the nuclear powers to abandon the out-of-date thinking of the Cold War period and take a fresh look. Above all, I appeal to them to bear in mind the long-term threat that nuclear weapons pose to humankind and to begin action towards their elimination. Remember your duty to humanity.

My second appeal is to my fellow scientists. I described earlier the disgraceful role played by a few scientists, caricatured as 'Dr Strangeloves,'[5] in fueling the arms race. They did great damage to the image of science.

On the other side there are the scientists, in Pugwash and other bodies, who devote much of their time and ingenuity to averting the dangers created by advances in science and technology. However, they embrace only a small part of the scientific community. I want to address the scientific community as a whole.

You are doing fundamental work, pushing forward the frontiers of knowledge, but often you do it without giving much thought to the impact of your work on society. Precepts such as 'science is neutral' or 'science has nothing to do with politics,' still prevail. They are remnants of the ivory tower mentality, although the ivory tower was finally demolished by the Hiroshima bomb.

Here, for instance, is a question: Should any scientist work on the development of weapons of mass destruction? A clear "no" was the answer recently given by Hans Bethe. Professor Bethe, a Nobel laureate, is the most senior of the surviving members of the Manhattan Project.[6] On the occasion of the 50th Anniversary of Hiroshima, he issued a statement that I will quote in full.

As the Director of the Theoretical Division at Los Alamos, I participated at the most senior level in the World War II Manhattan Project that produced the first atomic weapons.

Now, at age 88, I am one of the few remaining such senior persons alive. Looking back at the half century since that time, I feel the most intense relief that these weapons have

*not been used since World War II, mixed with the horror
that tens of thousands of such weapons have been built
since that time - one hundred times more than any of us at
Los Alamos could ever had imagined.*

*Today we are rightly in an era of disarmament and dis-
mantlement of nuclear weapons. But in some countries
nuclear weapons development still continues. Whether and
when the various Nations of the World can agree to stop
this is uncertain. But individual scientists can still influ-
ence this process by withholding their skills.*

*Accordingly, I call on all scientists in all countries to cease
and desist from work creating, developing, improving and
manufacturing further nuclear weapons - and, for that
matter, other weapons of potential mass destruction such as
chemical and biological weapons.*

If all scientists heeded this call there would be no more
new nuclear warheads; no French scientists at Mururoa:[7]
no new chemical and biological poisons. The arms race
would be truly over.

But there are other areas of scientific research that may
directly or indirectly lead to harm to society. This calls for constant vigilance. The purpose of some government or industrial
research is sometimes concealed, and misleading information
is presented to the public. It should be the duty of scientists to
expose such malfeasance. "Whistle-blowing" should become
part of the scientist's ethos. This may bring reprisals; a price
to be paid for one's convictions. The price may be very heavy,
as illustrated by the disproportionately severe punishment of
Mordechai Vanunu.[8] I believe he has suffered enough.

The time has come to formulate guidelines for the ethical conduct of scientist, perhaps in the form of a voluntary

Hippocratic Oath. This would be particularly valuable for young scientists when they embark on a scientific career. The US Student Pugwash Group has taken up this idea - and that is very heartening.

At a time when science plays such a powerful role in the life of society, when the destiny of the whole of mankind may hinge on the results of scientific research, it is incumbent on all scientists to be fully conscious of that role, and conduct themselves accordingly. I appeal to my fellow scientists to remember their responsibility to humanity.

My third appeal is to my fellow citizens in all countries: Help us to establish lasting peace in the world.

I have to bring to your notice a terrifying reality: with the development of nuclear weapons Man has acquired, for the first time in history, the technical means to destroy the whole of civilization in a single act. Indeed, the whole human species is endangered, by nuclear weapons or by other means of wholesale destruction which further advances in science are likely to produce.

I have argued that we must eliminate nuclear weapons. While this would remove the immediate threat, it will not provide permanent security. Nuclear weapons cannot be disinvented. The knowledge of how to make them cannot be erased. Even in a nuclear-weapon-free world, should any of the great powers become involved in a military confrontation, they would be tempted to rebuild their nuclear arsenals. That would still be a better situation than the one we have now, because the rebuilding would take a considerable time, and in that time the dispute might be settled. A nuclear-weapon-free world would be safer than the present one. But the danger of the ultimate catastrophe would still be there.

The only way to prevent it is to abolish war altogether. War must cease to be an admissible social institution. We must learn to resolve our disputes by means other than military confrontation.

This need was recognized forty years ago when we said in the Russell- Einstein Manifesto:

Here then is the problem which we present to you, stark and dreadful, and inescapable: shall we put an end to the human race: or shall mankind renounce war?

The abolition of war is also the commitment of the nuclear weapon states: Article VI of the NPT calls for a treaty on general and complete disarmament under strict and effective international control.

Any international treaty entails some surrender of national sovereignty, and is generally unpopular. As we said in the Russell-Einstein Manifesto: *"The abolition of war will demand distasteful limitations of national sovereignty."* Whatever system of governance is eventually adopted, it is important that it carries the people with it. We need to convey the message that safeguarding our common property, humankind, will require developing in each of us a new loyalty: a loyalty to mankind. It calls for the nurturing of a feeling of belonging to the human race. We have to become world citizens.

Notwithstanding the fragmentation that has occurred since the end of the Cold War, and the many wars for recognition of national or ethnic identities, I believe that the prospects for the acceptance of this new loyalty are now better than at the time of the Russell-Einstein Manifesto. This is so largely because of the enormous progress made by science and technology during these 40 years. The fantastic advances in communication and transportation have shrunk our globe. All nations of the world have become close neighbors. Modern information techniques enable us to learn instantly about every event in every part of the globe. We can talk to each other via the various networks. This facility will improve enormously with time, because the achievements so far have only scratched the surface. Technology is driving us together. In many ways we are becoming like one family.

In advocating the new loyalty to mankind I am not suggesting that we give up national loyalties. Each of us has loyalties to several groups - from the smallest, the family, to the largest, at present, the nation. Many of these groups provide protection for their members. With the global threats resulting from science and technology, the whole of humankind now needs protection. We have to extend our loyalty to the whole of the human race.

What we are advocating in Pugwash, a war-free world, will be seen by many as a Utopian dream. It is not Utopian. There already exist in the world large regions, for example, the European Union, within which war is inconceivable. What is needed is to extend these to cover the world's major powers.

In any case, we have no choice. The alternative is unacceptable. Let me quote the last passage of the Russell-Einstein Manifesto:

> *We appeal, as human beings, to human beings: Remember your humanity and forget the rest. If you can do so, the way lies open for a new paradise; if you cannot, there lies before you the risk of universal death.*

The quest for a war-free world has a basic purpose: survival. But if in the process we learn how to achieve it by love rather than by fear, by kindness rather than by compulsion; if in the process we learn to combine the essential with the enjoyable, the expedient with the benevolent, the practical with the beautiful, this will be an extra incentive to embark on this great task.

Above all, remember your humanity.

---

1. Baron Solly Zuckerman of Burnham Thorpe, Norfolk, held a number of such governmental appointments during World War II and after.

2. More recently, in the Pugwash Newsletter of October 1998 Rotblat refers to a recently leaked secret Presidential Decision Directive outlining nuclear strategy, which requires the retention of nuclear weapons for the foreseeable future as a basis for the national security of the United States.

3. In 1962 the Soviet Union moved to install nuclear missiles in Cuba in order to deter any attack on Cuba by the United States. The United States demanded that the missiles be withdrawn, and both the United States and the Soviet Union were on the brink of a nuclear war. However, Nikita Khrushchev, Soviet premier and first secretary of the Communist Party, agreed to withdraw the missiles, and the crisis passed.

4. Rotblat refers to the Pugwash volume, Verification: Monitoring Disarmament, (1991), written and edited by high calibre experts from both the West and the Soviet Union, which illustrates how Pugwash scientists of different ideological backgrounds could cooperate in approaching a sensitive security issue. See Selected Bibliography below.

5. The 1964 black comedy anti-war film about the dropping of the bomb was entitled "Dr. Strangelove Or How I Stopped Worrying and Learned to Love the Bomb".

6. Hans Albrecht Bethe, born in Germany in 1906, resettled in the United States in 1935 to teach at Cornell University. He was at Los Alamos from 1943-46, and in 1958 he was scientific adviser to the United States at the nuclear test ban talks in Geneva. In 1967 he was awarded the Nobel Prize in Physics "for

his contributions to the theory of nuclear reactions, especially his discoveries concerning the energy production in stars".

7. The South Pacific atoll of Mururoa in French Polynesia was the site of a series of French underwater nuclear bomb tests, which began in 1995 and ended in January 1996.

8. An Israeli technician, working at the Demona nuclear reactor, felt that Israel's secret production of plutonium there for nuclear weapons should be known by Israelis and the world, and as a matter of conscience he made the information public in 1985. He was lured to Rome by Israeli secret agents, kidnapped and brought back to Israel where he was secretly tried, convicted, and sentenced to eighteen years in prison. He spent at least the first 12 years in solitary confinement, while a worldwide campaign continued for his liberation. Adopted as a prisoner of conscience by Amnesty International, he has often been nominated for the Nobel Peace Prize.

Appendix D

ABOLITION 2000
FOUNDING STATEMENT
April 1995

A secure and livable world for our children and grandchildren and all future generations requires that we achieve a world free of nuclear weapons and redress the environmental degradation and human suffering that is the legacy of fifty years of nuclear weapons testing and production.

Further, the inextricable link between the "peaceful" and warlike uses of nuclear technologies and the threat to future generations inherent in creation and use of long-lived radioactive materials must be recognized. We must move toward reliance on clean, safe, renewable forms of energy production that do not provide the materials for weapons of mass destruction and do not poison the environment for thousands of centuries. The true "inalienable" right is not to nuclear energy, but to life, liberty and security of person in a world free of nuclear weapons.

We recognize that a nuclear weapons free world must be achieved carefully and in a step by step manner. We are convinced of its technological feasibility. Lack of political will, especially on the part of the nuclear weapons states, is the only true barrier. As chemical and biological weapons are prohibited, so must nuclear weapons be prohibited.

We call upon all states particularly the nuclear weapons states, declared and de facto to take the following steps to achieve nuclear weapons abolition. We further urge the states parties to the NPT to demand binding commitments by the declared nuclear weapons states to implement these measures:

1. Initiate immediately and conclude[*] negotiations on a nuclear weapons abolition convention that requires the phased elimination of all nuclear weapons within a timebound framework, with provisions for effective verification and enforcement.[**]
2. Immediately make an unconditional pledge not to use or threaten to use nuclear weapons.
3. Rapidly complete a truly comprehensive test ban treaty with a zero threshold and with the stated purpose of precluding nuclear weapons development by all states.
4. Cease to produce and deploy new and additional nuclear weapons systems, and commence to withdraw and disable deployed nuclear weapons systems.
5. Prohibit the military and commercial production and reprocessing of all weapons-usable radioactive materials.
6. Subject all weapons-usable radioactive materials and nuclear facilities in all states to international accounting, monitoring, and safeguards, and estab-

lish a public international registry of all weapons-usable radioactive materials.

7. Prohibit nuclear weapons research, design, development, and testing through laboratory experiments including but not limited to non-nuclear hydrodynamic explosions and computer simulations, subject all nuclear weapons laboratories to international monitoring, and close all nuclear test sites.

8. Create additional nuclear weapons free zones such as those established by the treaties of Tlatelolco and Raratonga.

9. Recognize and declare the illegality of threat or use of nuclear weapons, publicly and before the World Court.

10. Establish an international energy agency to promote and support the development of sustainable and environmentally safe energy sources.

11. Create mechanisms to ensure the participation of citizens and NGOs in planning and monitoring the process of nuclear weapons abolition.

A world free of nuclear weapons is a shared aspiration of humanity. This goal cannot be achieved in a non-proliferation regime that authorizes the possession of nuclear weapons by a small group of states. Our common security requires the complete elimination of nuclear weapons. Our objective is definite and unconditional abolition of nuclear weapons.

---

*The 1995 Abolition 2000 Statement called for the conclusion of negotiations on a Nuclear Weapons Convention "by the year 2000." Recognizing that the nuclear weapons states would likely fail in their obligations to conclude such negotiations, this phrase was removed at the end of the year 2000 after member organizations voted and agreed upon its removal.

** The convention should mandate irreversible disarmament measures, including but not limited to the following: withdraw and disable all deployed nuclear weapons systems; disable and dismantle warheads; place warheads and weapon-usable radioactive materials under international safeguards; destroy ballistic missiles and other delivery systems. The convention could also incorporate the measures listed above which should be implemented independently without delay. When fully implemented, the convention would replace the NPT.

About the Nuclear Age
Peace Foundation

The Nuclear Age Peace Foundation is a non-profit, non-partisan international organization. Since 1982, it has initiated and supported worldwide efforts to enhance both global and human security and is a voice for millions of people concerned about the fate of the planet. The Foundation has consultative status to the United Nations Economic and Social Council and is recognized by the UN as a Peace Messenger Organization.

Vision
Our vision is a just and peaceful world, free of nuclear weapons.

Mission
To educate and advocate for peace and a world free of nuclear weapons, and to empower peace leaders.

Contact
Nuclear Age Peace Foundation
PMB 121, 1187 Coast Village Road, Suite 1
Santa Barbara, CA 93108-2794

Telephone: (805) 965-3443
Fax: (805) 568-0466
E-mail: wagingpeace@napf.org

Web Presence
We invite you to learn more about the Foundation's programs by visiting our websites.

www.wagingpeace.org
www.nuclearzero.org | www.nuclearfiles.org

About the Author

David Krieger is a founder of the Nuclear Age Peace
Foundation and has served as President of the Foundation since 1982. He has lectured throughout the United
States, Europe and Asia on issues of peace, security, international law, and the abolition of nuclear weapons. He
serves as an advisor to many peace organizations around
the world and has received many awards for his work for
a more peaceful and nuclear weapon-free world. He is a
graduate of Occidental College, and holds M.A. and Ph.D.
degrees in Political Science from the University of Hawaii
and a J.D. from the Santa Barbara College of Law.

Notes

1. Kuznick, Peter, "The Decision to Risk the Future: Harry Truman, the Atomic Bomb and the Apocalyptic Narrative," Nuclear Age Peace Foundation, http://www.wagingpeace. org/articles/2007/07/23_decision_to_risk.htm. Kuznick writes, "The fact that the bomb project had generated so much momentum by the time Truman became president that it would have taken bold leadership on his part to avoid using these new weapons has led some observers to minimize his personal responsibility. On several occasions, Groves insisted that Truman was swept along by the tide of events."
2. The clause was drafted by John J. McCloy, an Assistant Secretary of War under Henry Stimson, http://nuclearfiles.org/menu/ library/biographies/bio_mccloy-john.htm
3. The final text of Article 12 of the Potsdam Declaration made no mention of the Japanese emperor and stated: "The occupying forces of the Allies shall be withdrawn from Japan as soon as these objectives have been accomplished and there has been established in accordance with the freely expressed will of the Japanese people a peacefully inclined and responsible government."

4. LeFebre, Walter, "Interview," American Experience, http:// www.pbs.org/wgbh/americanexperience/features/inter- view/truman-lafeber/

5. Chen, C. Peter, "Harry Truman," World War II Database, http://ww2db.com/person_bio.php?person_id=105

6. Long, Doug, "Hiroshima: Was It Absolutely Necessary?" http://www.spectacle.org/696/long.html

7. Ibid.

8. Eisenhower, Dwight, "Ike on Ike," Newsweek, November 11, 1963.

9. Weber, Mark, "Was Hiroshima Necessary?" Institute for Historical Review, http://www.ihr.org/jhr/v16/v16n3p-4_ Weber.html

10. Leahy, William, I Was There, New York: Whittlesey House, 1950, p. 441.

11. "Einstein to Roosevelt, August 2, 1939," http://www.dannen. com/ae-fdr.html. All of Einstein's letters to Roosevelt are online at http://hypertextbook.com/eworld/einstein.shtml

12. Szilard, Leo, "President Truman Did Not Understand," U.S. News and World Report, August 15, 1960, http://members. peak.org/~danneng/decision/usnews.html

13. Einstein, Albert, "Albert Einstein Quotes, Finest Quotes," http://www.finestquotes.com/author_quotes-author- Albert%20Einstein-page-5.htm

14. Matsubara, Miyoko "The Spirit of Hiroshima," http://www. wagingpeace.org/articles/1999/00/00_matsubara_spirit- hiroshima.php

15. Blackman, Christine, "The chance of nuclear war is greater than you think: Stanford engineer makes risk analysis," Stan- ford Report 17, July 17, 2009, http://news.stanford.edu/ news/2009/july22/hellman-nuclear-analysis-071709.html

16. On numbers of nuclear weapons in the world, see SIPRI Yearbook 2011, Chapter 7, "World Nuclear Forces," Stock-

holm International Peace Research Institute, http://www.
sipri.org/yearbook/2011/07

17. Obama, Barack, "Remarks of President Barack Obama,"
Hradcany Square, Czech Republic, April 5, 2009, Embassy of
the United States, Prague, Czech Republic, http://prague.
usembassy.gov/obama.html

18. Ibid.

19. Ibid.

20. Ibid.

21. United Nations General Assembly Resolution I(1), "Estab-
lishment of a Commission to Deal with the Problems Raised
by the Discovery of Atomic Energy," http://www.icanw.
org/1946

22. "The Baruch Plan," Atomic Archive, http://www.atomi-
carchive.com/Docs/Deterrence/BaruchPlan.shtml

23. "Nuremberg Trial Proceedings, Vol. 1, Charter of the International Military Tribunal," Yale Law School, Lillian Goldman
Law Library, http://avalon.law.yale.edu/imt/imtconst.asp

24. "Einstein to Roosevelt, August 2, 1939," http://www.dannen.
com/ae-fdr.html

25. "The Manhattan Project, Imagining the Bomb," Atomic
Energy and Nuclear History Learning Curriculum, http://
osulibrary.oregonstate.edu/specialcollections/omeka/
exhibits/show/atomic/manhattan/imagining

26. The Manhattan Project Heritage Preservation Association,
http://www.mphpa.org/classic/COTMP/quote_submit.
htm

27. "The Emergency Committee of Atomic Scientists," The Pauling Blog, http://paulingblog.wordpress.com/2010/08/04/
the-emergency-committee-of-atomic-scientists/

28. "The Russell-Einstein Manifesto," Issued in London, July
9, 1955, The Pugwash Conferences on Science and World
Affairs, http://www.pugwash.org/about/manifesto.htm

29. Ibid.

30. Ibid.

31. "Leo Szilard," Absolute Astronomy, http://www.absoluteastronomy.com/topics/Le%C3%B3_Szil%C3%A1rd

32. Wells, H. G., The Last War, A World Set Free, Lincoln: University of Nebraska Press, 2001.

33. "Today in History: December 2, 1942," Library of Congress, American Memory, http://memory.loc.gov/ammem/today/dec02.html

34. "Leo Szilard," Leo Szilard and the Atomic Bomb, http://www.doug-long.com/szilard.htm

35. Alperovitz, Gar, "More on Atomic Diplomacy," Bulletin of the Atomic Scientists, December 1985, http://coursesa.matrix.msu.edu/~hst203/readings/alperovitz.html

36. "Report of the Committee on Political and Social Problems," Manhattan Project "Metallurgical Laboratory," University of Chicago, June 11, 1945, http://www.dannen.com/decision/franck.html

37. "The Manhattan Project: Making the Atomic Bomb," Atomic Archive, http://www.atomicarchive.com/History/mp/chronology.shtml.

38. "A Petition to the President of the United States," July 17, 1945, U.S. National Archives, Record Group 77, Records of the Chief of Engineers, Manhattan Engineer District, Harrison-Bundy File, folder #76, http://www.dannen.com/decision/45-07-17.html.

39. Ibid.

40. Harrison, Guy P., "The scientist who said 'no,'" The Caymanian Compass, September 21, 2005, http://www.pugwash.org/publication/obits/obit-rotblat-cayman-article.pdf.

41. Rotblat, Joseph, "Remember Your Humanity," Nobel Lecture, December 10, 1995, http://www.nobelprize.org/nobel_prizes/peace/laureates/1995/rotblat-lecture.html.

42. Ibid.

43. Ibid

44. Krieger, David, "Nuclear Weapons and the University of California," Nuclear Age Peace Foundation, July 26, 2007, http://www.wagingpeace.org/articles/2007/07/26_krieger_nuc_weapons_and_UC.htm.

45. Taue, Tomihisa, "Nagasaki Peace Declaration," August 9, 2007, http://www.acronym.org.uk/docs/0708/doc07.htm.

46. Goodall, Jane, "Remembering the Marshall Islands," http://www.pacificpeoplespartnership.org/marshallislands.html.

47. "United States Nuclear Tests, July 1945 through September 1992," U.S. Department of Energy, Nevada Operations Office, DOE/NV—209-REV 15, December 2000, http://www.nv.doe.gov/library/publications/historical/DOENV_209_REV15.pdf.

48. Caldicott, Helen, Missile Envy, New York: William Morrow & Co., 1984.

49. The US today maintains some 50 nuclear weapons in Turkey, one of five NATO member countries to allow US nuclear weapons on its soil.

50. Pauling, Linus, No More War!, New York: Dodd, Mead & Company, 1983.

51. "Israel's Nuclear Weapon Capability: An Overview," The Risk Report, July-August 1996, http://www.wisconsinproject.org/countries/israel/nuke.html.

52. Helfand, Ira, "Nuclear Famine: Two Billion People at Risk," Somerville, MA: International Physicians for the Prevention of Nuclear War (IPPNW), http://www.ippnw.org/pdf/nuclear-famine-two-billion-at-risk-2013.pdf

53. MacPherson, James, "Minot chief sets bar high after nuke gaffe," Air Force Times, February 2, 2008, http://www.airforcetimes.com/news/2008/02/ap_nukemistake_080202/.

54. Gofman, John and Arthur Tamplin, "Why We Challenged the Atomic Energy Commission," Bulletin of the Atomic

Scientists, September 1971, http://www.airforcetimes.com/
news/2008/02/ap_nukemistake_080202/.

55. "Best Quotes on Nuclear Weapons Policy," The Reagan
Vision for a Nuclear-Weapons-Free World, http://www.
thereaganvision.org/best-nuclear-quotes/.

56. Treaty on the Non-Proliferation of Nuclear Weapons, United
Nations Office for Disarmament Affairs, http://www.un.org/
disarmament/WMD/Nuclear/NPT.shtml.

57. Legality of the Threat or Use of Nuclear Weapons, International Court of Justice, Advisory Opinion, July 8, 1996,
http://www.icj-cij.org/docket/index.php?p1=3&p2=4&k=e
1&p3=4&case=95.

58. Graham, Thomas and Max Kampelman, "Commentary:
Restoring U.S. nuclear-free leadership," The Washington
Times, April 2, 2008, http://www.washingtontimes.com/
news/2008/apr/02/commentary-restoring-us-nuclear-free-
leadership/?page=all.

59. "U.S. 'Negative Security Assurances' at a Glance," Arms Control Association, http://www.armscontrol.org/factsheets/
negsec.

60. Phillips, Alan F., "20 Mishaps that Might Have Started Accidental Nuclear War," January, 1998, Nuclear Age Peace Foundation, https://www.wagingpeace.org/articles/1998/01/00_
phillips_20-mishaps.php.

61. Convention on the Prohibition of the Development, Production, Stockpiling and Use of Chemical Weapons and on their
Destruction, Organization for the Prohibition of Chemical
Weapons, http://www.opcw.org/chemical-weapons-conven-
tion/.

62. Convention on the Prohibition of the Development, Production and Stockpiling of Bacteriological (Biological) and
Toxin Weapons and Their Destruction, The Biological and
Toxin Weapons Convention Website, http://www.opbw.
org/.

63. Nuclear Weapons Convention, The Lawyers Committee on Nuclear Policy, Inc., http://lcnp.org/mnwc/.

64. "Letter from Nancy Reagan," Nuclear Security Project, October 4, 2007, http://www.nuclearsecurityproject.org/media/letter-from-nancy-reagan.

65. Reagan, Ronald, "Address Before a Joint Session of the Congress on the State of the Union," The American Presidency Project, January 24, 1984, http://www.presidency.ucsb.edu/ws/index.php?pid=40205#axzz1iiM8QN5s.

66. "Letter from Nancy Reagan," Nuclear Security Project, October 4, 2007, http://www.nuclearsecurityproject.org/media/letter-from-nancy-reagan.

67. Lettow, Paul, Ronald Reagan and His Quest to Abolish Nuclear Weapons, New York: Random House, 2005, p. 75.

68. Ibid., p. 138.

69. "Letter from Nancy Reagan," Nuclear Security Project, October 4, 2007, http://www.nuclearsecurityproject.org/media/letter-from-nancy-reagan.

70. Information about the United Nations Millennium Development Goals can be found online at http://www.unmillenniumproject.org/.

71. The SIPRI Yearbook 2012, by the Stockholm International Peace Research Institute, states on page 8: "The world total [military expenditure] for 2011 is estimated to have been $1738 billion, representing 2.5 per cent of global gross domestic product or $249 for each person." The SIPRI Yearbook 2012 is online at http://www.sipri.org/yearbook/2012/files/SIPRIYB12Summary.pdf.

72. Camus, Albert, "Between Hell and Reason, Essays from the Resistance Newspaper Combat 1944 - 1947," Hanover, NH: Wesleyan University Press, 1991, pp. 110-111.

73. Krieger, David, "Sunflower Peace Day," Nuclear Age Peace Foundation, June 1996, http://www.wagingpeace.org/articles/2006/05/00_krieger_sunflower-day.htm.

74. A list of signers of "Santa Barbara Declaration: Reject Nuclear Deterrence: An Urgent Call to Action" can be found at http://www.wagingpeace.org/articles/db_article.php?article_id=209.

75. Roy, Arundhati, "The End of Imagination," Frontline, Vol. 15, No. 16, August 1 - 14, 1998, http://www.hindu.com/fline/fl1516/15160040.htm.

76. Ibid.

77. Roy, Arundhati, "Under the Nuclear Shadow," Irish Times, 2002, http://tehomet.net/arundhati.html.

78. Williams, Rachel and Richard Norton-Taylor, "Nuclear Submarines Collide in Atlantic," The Guardian, February 16, 2009.

79. Burdick, Eugene and Harvey Wheeler, Fail-Safe, Hopewell, NJ: Ecco Press, 1999.

80. Helfand, Ira, "Nuclear Famine: Two Billion People at Risk," Somerville, MA: International Physicians for the Prevention of Nuclear War (IPPNW), http://www.ippnw.org/pdf/nuclear-famine-two-billion-at-risk-2013.pdf

81. Kennedy, Robert, Thirteen Days, a Memoir of the Cuban Crisis, New York: W.W. Norton & Co., 1971.

82. Krieger, David, "Sunflowers: The Symbol of a World Free of Nuclear Weapons," http://www.ksdom.org/index_files/Page 8136.htm.

83. Isaacs, John, "Strategic Revelation," Bulletin of the Atomic Scientists, February 23, 2012, http://www.thebulletin.org/web-edition/features/strategic-revelation.

84. Butler, George Lee, "Nuclear Arms Could Bring Apocalypse," The Light Party, http://www.lightparty.com/Peace/Apocalypse.html.